Never Good Enough ...
UNTIL NOW

Best Wishes

Sheron Gardiner

Do you like to read?
Take a book, share a book
Enjoy! From **Judy and Patrick**

Never Good Enough...
UNTIL NOW

A TRUE STORY ABOUT SURVIVING LIFE IN THE HARD LANE

SHARON GARDINER

Copyright © 2012 by Sharon Gardiner.

Library of Congress Control Number:		2012901993
ISBN:	Hardcover	978-1-4691-6121-1
	Softcover	978-1-4691-6120-4
	Ebook	978-1-4691-6122-8

All rights reserved. No part of this book may be reproduced or transmitted in any form or by any means, electronic or mechanical, including photocopying, recording, or by any information storage and retrieval system, without permission in writing from the copyright owner.

To order additional copies of this book, contact:
Xlibris Corporation
1-800-618-969
www.Xlibris.com.au
Orders@Xlibris.com.au

Contents

Chapter 1	The Birth of a Pearl—Where it All Started	13
Chapter 2	The Innocence of Childhood—We are Little Children	23
Chapter 3	My Family Story—The Generations	28
Chapter 4	Shattered Memories—The Trauma of Domestic Violence	34
Chapter 5	Raw Fear—A Scarred Child	37
Chapter 6	An Era of Misguided Discipline—Society Got it Wrong	40
Chapter 7	My Mother's Messages—Inconsistency and Confusion	43
Chapter 8	Independence—Hiding Under the Radar	48
Chapter 9	Looking for Love—In all the Wrong Places	50
Chapter 10	Booze, Sex, and Barely Seventeen—Like a Bull in a China Shop	57
Chapter 11	Emotional Wounds Need Healing Too—A Nurturing Profession	61
Chapter 12	Relationships—The Picket Fence	69
Chapter 13	My Father's Last Days—A Cruel Twist	75
Chapter 14	The Fairy Tale—Till Death Do Us Part	82
Chapter 15	The Penny Dropped—This Started the Wheels of Change	87
Chapter 16	Self Doubt Overtook Me—Again	97
Chapter 17	On the Job—A Surreal Experience	106
Chapter 18	A Diagnosis of Depression—My Resistance	109
Chapter 19	A Dark Time—A Place Never Revisited	112
Chapter 20	A Shared Story—Brings a Sense of Relief	116
Chapter 21	What Can I Learn—Knowledge Feeds Us	121

Chapter 22	The Ultimate Sacrifice—No Place for Judgement	125
Chapter 23	The Police Family—A Special Bond	130
Chapter 24	A Trip to Self Discovery—Where Did I Go	134
Chapter 25	The Pain behind the Smile—My Secret	141
Chapter 26	Always Their Mother—Always Her Children	145
Chapter 27	Feeling Like a Million Dollars—An Unfamiliar Feeling	148
Chapter 28	People Worse Off—They are Everywhere	153
Chapter 29	Life is Precious—Gone at Fifty	157
Chapter 30	Grief is a Personal Thing—Do It Your Way	160
Chapter 31	Slow Steps in a Forward Direction—A Snail's Pace	162
Chapter 32	A Christmas to Forget—So Many Memories	169
Chapter 33	The Irony of the Job—Another Shared Moment	173
Chapter 34	The Illusion of Family—My Angel Landlord	175
Chapter 35	Always Room for Family—You Just Have to Make It!	179
Chapter 36	The Stress of the Job—Life is Fragile	184
Chapter 37	The Importance of Prevention—A Supportive Environment	192
Chapter 38	Tucking my Childhood into Bed—For Good	199
Chapter 39	A Letter to My Mother—I Have Always Loved You	207
Chapter 40	Domestic Violence—An Undesirable Prerequisite	211
Chapter 41	History Can Repeat Itself—If We Let It	217
Chapter 42	The Gift of a New Beginning—The Gift is to Myself	220

Important Phone Numbers and Resources 227

DEDICATION

To my daughter and son,
My heart is so full of love for you both.
You are my pearls and I am so proud of you both.

I would also like to dedicate this book to all those people out there who are experiencing adversity and need that little bit of inspiration to get them through. You will be OK.

DISCLAIMER

The opinions, beliefs and views of the author are personal and in no way representative of that of the NSW Police Service, Department of Community Services (DOCS), or NSW Health in relation to nursing services. This book gives general advice and should not be substituted for professional help. At the back of this book I have provided a list of organisations where people can seek help and support. Some of the stories in this book have been adapted to protect the identity of individuals.

ACKNOWLEDGEMENT

Parts of this story were written in a little granny flat that I called home for five months. To Sonny my angel landlord, I thank you from the bottom of my heart.

This book would not have been written if it wasn't for the support and encouragement I received from my dear friends Kristy and Stacey. My life has been so much richer with the two of you by my side.

Not only did you support me through the most difficult times in my life but you also believed in me every step of the way.

To my dearest friends who support me in all areas of my life—I appreciate all that you do for me. Sue, you are my rock and may we have another forty years of friendship. Alice, our souls are connected whilst on our individual journeys, we will get there.

A special message to Robyn—(my long time boss) you are a special person and I sincerely thank you for all that you have done for me.

Thank you to all those inspirational people who have written so many meaningful quotes that I have used throughout the content of this book. Your quotes gave me hope and inspiration during the time I needed it most.

I feel privileged to have had so many special people in my life both past and present who have taught me so many lessons and supported me during my darkest times. You know who you are. Thank you.

My sincere thanks and appreciation go to those of you who gave me valuable feedback during the early stages of my writing. Thank you for being so generous with your time and thoughts. It has been a long process but I did it.

I would not have been able to achieve so much in my life without the support from two very professional ladies named Sue and Marianne. You helped me navigate the roller coaster of life. My heartfelt thanks and gratitude go to you both.

Lastly, my sincere thanks go to the wonderfully dedicated people at Xlibris. You took my manuscript in its raw form and turned it into this beautiful book. You believed in my story and helped me realise my dream. A special thanks to Dori—you are amazing.

CHAPTER 1

THE BIRTH OF A PEARL—WHERE IT ALL STARTED

> Personal growth can be painful, because it can make us feel ashamed and humiliated to face our own darkness. But our spiritual goal is the journey out of fear based, painful mental patterns, to those of love and peace.
>
> (Marianne Williamson)

A new baby can be likened to a pearl, being seen for the first time as the fisherman opens the clam that encapsulates it. The pearl is created perfect regardless of its shape and size. It does not need to be altered but instead is highly sought after due to its natural beauty.

I cannot recall my own birth or any stories around my arriving in the world; however, I can remember the birth of my children. Their birth was highly anticipated. The nine months seemed to drag on as I impatiently waited their entry into the world. As a nurse, I knew that they would enter the world by sliding through a birth passage towards an opening no bigger than a rockmelon. When my children did arrive and took their first breath of life and screamed to the world 'I'm here', their cry was music to my ears.

When I look back on this, I realise how frightened they might have been . . . all the noise, the bright lights, people rushing around. They, like me, were only comforted when pressed against the warm skin of their mother and soothed by the voice of someone who loved them.

When I held my children for the first time, tears of joy and happiness rolled down my face. My heart and soul became filled with so much love that I thought I was floating on air. I remember looking at them and being struck by their bright inquisitive eyes and their perfection. As they grew, I watched them absorb the world that surrounded them. They kicked their feet, waved their arms about, and grabbed whatever was nearby. They laughed and chuckled at the sensation of warm hands tickling their soft unblemished skin.

As I watched them, I was struck by their innocence and realised that everything was a new experience to them. This innocence is abundant in all babies, and as their range of experiences increase, their lives slowly begin to change.

The first significant changes during early childhood are introduced to us by our caregivers. These are the people who are entrusted to care for us and teach us about the world and ourselves. Some caregivers educate themselves as they take care of us while others try to learn as much as they can before we arrive in the world. There are some who take the chance that what they know is enough. Others choose to model their parenting on how they have been parented themselves.

As babies, our future is in the hands of our caregivers and what we learn about ourselves, and the world comes from what they teach us. Of course, some of what they teach us is important because they want us to be safe and grow. They teach us how our bodies work, how to get on with other people, how to behave appropriately and hopefully, how to survive in a sometimes harsh world. This is not what I was taught.

I remember my first day at a new school. I was six years old and full of hope. I left home that morning feeling excited about what lay ahead of me . . . new friends, new environment, new things to learn as well as fun and adventure. What I found was very different.

Standing alone on the school veranda, I watched the other children play and I stood waiting for them to ask me to join them. Instead, they started calling out, 'Freckle face, freckle face, you are a freckle face.' I remember thinking why a few freckles on my face made me unworthy of playing with the other children. I can still remember the pain and disappointment of that moment, even forty-six years later.

I was also confused by their words because my mother had referred to my freckles as 'sun kisses', which made me think they were something special. My first day at that school taught me that not everyone saw my freckles as special. Instead, I realised they made me look different from the other children and I started to learn to dislike them and worked to 'remove' them.

After school that day, I came home to my grandmother and told her what had happened. My grandmother was very resourceful because she grew up in England and had lived through the First World War and the great depression in the 1930s. I asked her how I could get rid of my freckles or at least fade them. She told me to rub fresh tomatoes over my face, telling me the natural acidity in the tomatoes would fade my freckles.

So what do you think I did?

If you said that I rubbed tomatoes over my freckles, you're right. Every day, I rubbed my face and anxiously waited for my freckles to disappear. As you can imagine, it didn't work. Today, I still have them not just on my face but all over my body. The only remedy that stops them from increasing and becoming darker is liberal layers of sunscreen, whilst the daily use of make-up helps to disguise them.

To me, school was a harsh place, which is why the stability of my home environment was so important for me. I believe that a home should meet our basic needs such as food and shelter. It should also provide us with a feeling of security and caregivers that support and guide us. In addition to this, I believe that a home should be a place where behind closed doors you could be yourself and be accepted for who you are, unconditionally.

To me, unconditional love is just that. It means loving and being loved no matter what happens. As babies, we look to our caregivers for this unconditional love. We connect with them through eye contact and physical interactions such as hugs, being held close, and soothing caresses. This attachment to our main caregivers forms the basis of our future relationships and how we see ourselves as individuals.

In those early years, these connections are the source of one's survival, so we adapt our behaviours in order to gain greater connections. As we grow older, we learn to meet some of our own survival needs and become less reliant on our caregivers. Our attachment therefore becomes more emotionally based. We discover that whilst unconditional love was free flowing in our earlier years, that as we get older, our relationship with our caregivers can change. We start to form new relationships, and as we do that we turn to the stability and safety of our homes to help us cope effectively in the real world where we are no longer protected.

As we grow, we absorb a barrage of information from everything around us, in particular within our homes. What we learn, we put into practice in the real world and we find ourselves mirroring the behaviours of our caregivers and significant others. In terms of developing our survival skills, we hope and pray, with fingers crossed, that these individuals have got some idea of what they are doing. We can only hope that they have learnt from the mistakes of their caregivers and will not repeat them.

It's all a bit risky, wouldn't you say?

We don't choose our parents or other caregivers, just as the pearl does not choose the clam; we are born to them. The lessons and support that we get from our parents and caregivers come from the things that have influenced them and the norms of society at the time. We know from history that both can sometimes get it wrong.

I have come to realise that my mother and father raised me the best way that they knew how and provided me with the skills that they believed would enable me to survive. My childhood connections with my parents and the experiences I had in my childhood are what have made me who I am and have provided me with the tools and strategies that I have used to survive.

Looking back, I believe that we learn our childhood lessons from our parents or caregivers with precision, but not necessarily with the wisdom, to effectively filter the good from the bad and the positive from the negative. The ability to do so comes as we mature; however, we can still hear the voices of our past causing difficulties throughout our adult lives.

At home I was frequently called 'little miss perfect', 'miss prissy', and 'little miss know it all'. I learnt from an early age that these names meant that I needed to be perfect, and I still today strive to achieve perfection in the things that I do.

Whilst I have some fond memories of my childhood, recalling the negative things seem to come easier to me, most likely because I can associate the negative with a traumatic event. I know there were fun times, and I have the photos to prove it. I sit and look at these photos but find it difficult to connect with that small child in the picture. Instead, it is the negative experiences and unkind words spoken to me that I remember most. It is like my subconscious holds on to these negative experiences, placing them in the 'top-draw', making them close at hand in case I need them.

I believe that the subconscious mind stores the negative experiences in an effort to protect us against any future negatives. It sort of makes us react in a way that has worked to keep us safe in the past. In other words, stores the survival strategy that we used to protect ourselves from a previous trauma.

I also believe that the negative comments and experiences alter our thinking patterns and how we behave. In my own memories of my adult life, I often and too readily only recall the bad and not the good, the negative and not the positive. That is, even though, I have proof that there were good times as well as positive experiences. This realisation has led me to spend a lot of time trying to work out why I continue to think in a negative way. I know for a fact, my life has had some extremely positive moments in the past and also the present.

So . . . is my thinking pattern just habitual, subconscious, or a reflection of the person I am?

I think for me as an adult, I underestimated the impact my childhood had on my development and my progression into adulthood. My memory of my childhood has been dominated by negative emotions such as fear, rejection, abandonment, insecurity, worry, instability, and aggression. These stored emotions are not my reality in the present time so why do I still give them any meaning.

This year my understanding of the past has caused me to focus on the more positive things that have happened in my life and prioritise my needs, desires, and wants.

I began the year by enlisting the help of a fitness coach named Graeme. I was seeing great results but about eight weeks into our weekly sessions, I sustained an injury. As a result of my injury, our training regime needed to be trimmed back until I recovered. I was worried about going backwards with my fitness and mentioned this to Graeme. He started to talk about my level of fitness that he noted on our first session.

Before he could finish what he was saying, I sensed that he was starting to pay me a compliment and say something positive about me. I became restless and felt a panicky feeling come over me. I avoided making eye contact with Graeme and felt my anxiety level overtake my concentration so I could no longer hear what he was saying. Later in the day, I tried to recall the conversation because I wanted to hear what Graeme had to say about me. In my attempt to recall the conversation, I realised that I had intentionally blocked out the positive comments he had made about me and therefore could not recall them.

I was disappointed in myself and asked myself, 'Why did I feel so uncomfortable and not want to hear good things about myself?'

I realised at that moment that years of focusing on the negative made it impossible for me to hear and focus on the positive. I found this fascinating because I felt that I worked hard all my life to seek out praise and approval from others, yet I chose not to listen to it.

I had always known that I felt uncomfortable, accepting compliments, so I thought more intently about that. I realised that on hearing a compliment, I would come back with some comment that immediately deflected the attention elsewhere. My conversation with Graeme highlighted something that I had subconsciously been doing for years, and in doing so, I had created opposing thoughts. On one hand I would seek out praise and on the other hand would deflect that same praise.

How confusing is that?

This experience with Graeme made me think about all the messages we send out about ourselves and the messages we receive from others.

It was the innocence of my friend's son, which reminded me recently of the importance of the messages we receive from others and the impact they can have. As a typical three-year-old, Quinn loves to learn new skills and his brain takes in new information like a dry sponge to a bucket of water. One morning he came into my room carrying a large heavy book in his arms. As I took hold of the book, that depicted his favourite train engine, Quinn jumped into bed with me and propped himself into a prime position against the pillows. It had been raining very loud and heavy the night before, so I asked him if he heard the rain. He did hear the rain, and then went on to tell me that he was scared and what he did at the time to stop himself from feeling scared. I watched him slide under the bedclothes until his head was covered with the sheets and quilt. I asked him if going under the quilt helped. He told me that it did. I explained to him that even though it was raining outside and it sounded loud and scary, that it couldn't hurt him because he was safe and dry in his room. This explanation seemed to ease him and he accepted what I had said.

It occurred to me later that my comments were aimed at reassuring Quinn. Instead of belittling his fears and telling Quinn that he was being stupid or not very brave, I eased his fears by sending out the message to Quinn that it was OK to be afraid.

My time with Quinn, since that night, caused me to reflect back on the messages I had received over the years. I started looking into the impact of these messages on the way we may think and how this in turn impacts on the way we might think about ourselves.

After much soul-searching and reading everything, I could find on self-awareness, self-esteem, and the impact words can have, I have identified my own patterns of thinking. These patterns over the years have influenced the way I see myself and how others see me.

I realised that when positive things were said to me or about me, I 'covered my ears' so as not to hear the compliments that came my way. I also realised that I censored only certain compliments. Those that came from friends, family, and strangers, I didn't often hear. However, those comments made by my work colleagues or peers were, in most cases, heard loud and clear.

I decided to take steps to change what I heard and to ensure that I focused on comments made by all those around me. I could now see that I was clearly missing out on the recognition of those most dear to me. I realised that like the character of Vivienne in my favourite movie 'Pretty Woman', that whilst others may be telling us that we are pretty, smart, and special, we remember only the bad stuff because it is easier to believe.

It has taken a long time to uncover what makes me tick but I have committed myself to taking my power back and controlling my own life. My experiences with Graeme and Quinn have brought me to the point of wanting to make improvements in my life, by changing the messages I not only received, but gave to others as well. I like this quote from the author of *Empower Yourself*, Clive Murphy, who said,

> *'if you are not happy with the way you feel, all you have to do is change the program'*

Murphy refers to all messages we receive and give out as programs, which we use when thinking about ourselves and those around us. Who we are is largely a result of the messages and lessons we have learnt from others, in particular those we love most. Our significant others teach us about ourselves as well as themselves. They also provide us with our morals, values, and ethics and can influence the decisions we make.

The need for me to create immediate change in my thinking came from a single statement made by Dr Phil McGraw in 2009.

On 6 August 2009, I went to Acer Arena in Sydney's Olympic Park to see Dr Phil. During his talk, he made the statement that

> 'Today is the last time you will experience the 6 August 2009 in your lifetime'.

He went on to say that never again will you live this day, so you better make the most of it and think about doing something positive in your life.

This statement was a wake-up call for me. His comment changed my perspective on life and it became clearer to me what I needed to do. I started making small changes to take back better control of my life and where I was heading. I began to listen to the messages I was telling myself and pay closer attention to my thoughts and actions. I wanted to know why I think the way I do about certain things and what beliefs did I have around those thoughts.

The journey since then has been unique to me as it is for every individual who embarks on changing themselves and their life.

CHAPTER 2

THE INNOCENCE OF CHILDHOOD—
WE ARE LITTLE CHILDREN

> Life affords no greater responsibility, no greater privilege than the raising of the next generation.
>
> (C. Everett Koop)

In the middle of the garden at my childhood home, my father had made a large, sturdy wooden swing. The swing was very tall and took pride position in the garden as you walked through the side gate of our house. I got so much pleasure from the swing and every day I would come home from school and swing to my heart's content. I was in the safe surroundings of the garden and was able to forget all the things that happened during my day at school.

I could be as carefree as I wanted and let my childhood imagination take over me. Whilst I sat on the swing, I thought of all the wonderful things in life like the fairy tales that told of the beautiful princess, being rescued by her prince. I left my worries behind as the swing took me forwards and backwards on an adventure that only I was to undertake. I could go wherever I wanted because everything in my life I created in my dreams or my imagination. My thoughts also centred on my family because they were all I thought I needed at the time. Whilst I enjoyed the freedom of the swinging motion, I would sing a nursery rhyme out loud.

The words went something like 'I love to go, a wandering, along the mountain track and as I go, I love to sing a knapsack on my back' I followed that with a partially improvised version of the chorus 'Valderi!' 'Valdera!' La La La La La

Those were the only words I knew, so I just repeated them over and over again, at the top of my voice. While I was on the swing, I can recall, seeing my mother looking out of the kitchen window. She appeared to me to be accepting of her young carefree dreamy daughter as she was going about her business in the kitchen.

Today when I read any information about childhood, I can see the idealistic views that childhood should be a time of innocence, where children are openly expected to explore their wonderful surrounds, absorb them, and learn from them. As children learn new skills, they become more refined at them. They can continue to practice them until they master the skill they so badly want to learn. Our caregivers are there to guide and nurture us during our development while we discover the great things life has to offer. Childhood and the memories it creates should be a time that we treasure. For some of us, it just does not measure up as a time that we remember fondly.

Recently whilst walking, I looked across the road and I saw a children's play area. It was empty at the time, so I stopped. I leaned over to stretch my legs and I saw a swing out of the corner of my eye.

The sight of the swing brought back those fond memories of the swing in my family garden. I summed up the seat to see if it would take my weight. I thought to myself,

'Maybe all that I needed was some fun on the swing'.

I sat on the swing, with the presumption that I could take myself back in time. I wanted to be at that moment in time when I did not seem to have a care in the world. Only this time, I was going to spare the neighbours my singing. I propelled myself forwards and backwards, whilst I pictured myself in my garden on the same swing my father had made.

To my disappointment and frustration, I could not find the same head space nor could I reproduce those same carefree feelings. Instead, my mind just continued to keep churning over to a point where I felt like I was going to dizzily fall off, on to the well-padded ground. I sat thinking about my life today, and how I felt so alone and unsupported. There was no mother at the window looking at me nor was there the family that I imagined living happily together like a dream come true.

My mind was full of thoughts about the care of my son, both financially and emotionally. I thought of the difficulty in working two jobs and trying to find time to care for my own needs. I contemplated my future, with barely enough time left, to work before retirement. I just kept thinking about the stresses and pressures of life. My mind was going crazy causing my level of frustration to heighten and as it did, the force of my swinging motion intensified. I even tried to block out my thoughts, by singing the same nursery rhyme louder and louder in my head, but it didn't work either. My desire to return to that carefree moment in time was quickly replaced by the thought of

> 'How did I get myself into this situation and where did my dreams go?'

> 'Why, did I feel so undeserving of all the good things I had in my life?'

> I took a deep breath and with a sigh, I thought to myself

'Oh, how times have changed and how my life has changed!'

Sadly I realised that my life had become so different to how I imagined it during those moments on the swing in my childhood garden. I started to wonder,

'What happened in my life from that time until now?'

'What happened to all that love and acceptance that was part of being born and present in my early years of childhood?'

'When did the messages I received during my childhood become so debilitating that at age fifty-one I would be sitting on a swing and be wondering. Not about that mountain track or knapsack on my back, but a lifetime of self loathing instead'

I knew life could be likened to a journey, which starts at childhood and weaves its way along the many bumpy roads and curves. It is the love, guidance, and role modelling from those important people around us in our childhood, which helps smooth the pathway for our transition into adulthood. As young adults, we begin to develop our own compass, which can help guide us to a definitive destination in our own lives. I felt I missed that direction because of the instability of my childhood. I left home early to get away from that same instability, and therefore naively travelled the bumps and curves with a feel my way approach instead.

That day on the swing as an adult some forty or so, years later, I realised that I could be the compass in my own life. It was time I gave way to the years of self loathing and started some self-loving instead. I felt I had no choice but to search for the answers into my past, and what better place to start was that same place that housed the swing and that is my childhood.

The first thing that popped into my head about my childhood was the fact that you cannot choose your parents. My parents could not choose their parents either, so the messages passed on during parenting are often generational. That could be a good thing or a disaster waiting to happen.

I have heard a lot of people make comments that you cannot change your past so just get over it and move on, but I think differently. I do agree with the fact that you cannot change your past, but I believe that we can certainly try to at least gain a better understanding of our past. Understanding the 'why' of our past can bring about change in us and opens up unlimited opportunities for our future. Knowledge empowers us to change the things from our past that no longer assist us but rather hold us back from the future. When I became enlightened by this concept I had no choice but to begin my search for answers. If I believed that it was my past that was holding me back, then I owed it to myself to delve into it.

'You can't heal what you refuse to confront' . . .

Unknown

CHAPTER 3

MY FAMILY STORY—THE GENERATIONS

> I know why families were created with all their imperfections. They humanize you. They are made to make you forget yourself occasionally, so that the beautiful balance of life is not destroyed.
>
> (Anais Nin)

I was born in March 1960 at my family home in West Ham, England and at the time of my birth I was the fourth child. There were my two brothers, the oldest was six years of age, the next was aged four and then I had an older sister age two.

About three weeks after my birth, I succumbed to an unknown illness and my mother was told that I was not expected to survive. In preparation for my death, I was christened in my cot by the local priest. Then, I guess everyone just waited until I took my last breath. I know little information about that time, but I obviously recovered because I am here to tell my story.

At the age of three, my family migrated to Sydney, Australia as did many other families in the 1960s. My maternal grandmother migrated with us, and we travelled by sea to Australia on a cruise ship called, the Oriana. My mother was pregnant during the long voyage, and soon after the ship docked in Sydney Harbour, my younger sister was born. It was 1963 when her birth brought the number of children in our family to five.

My family were temporarily accommodated at the Cabramatta Hostel for migrants until we were able to find rental accommodation. After a few years living on the northern beaches of Sydney, we were allocated a housing commission home in the outer western suburb of St Marys. The suburb was relatively underdeveloped, nestled amongst native bushland and vacant reserves and about one hour travel from the Sydney CBD. There was one public primary school and one public high school. Most of the neighbourhood children attended the local public school, so we got to know them all very quickly. Our playground, after school, often turned out to be the middle of the road or the local bushland. We all just fitted in like the other families doing the exact same thing day in and day out. Life was simple in those days.

My father was born in 1927 in New Mexico but had parents of Irish origin. He grew up on his family's farm in the Irish town of Skibbereen. He was a quiet individual who loved to tell Irish jokes and tales of leprechauns. It was his love of alcohol and in particular, Guinness beer that used to get him into trouble.

My father was two different men to me. One man that I loved and the other one I feared. The father I loved was a funny and caring man who was easy-going. He liked woodwork and was a loyal dog lover.

We had several pet dogs throughout my childhood. I remember that sometimes we would have too many dogs to feed. The dog food was expensive therefore my father would choose, which dogs would be given up to the pound. Then he would take the dogs away and return alone. The pound was a long way away and one day, one of the dogs returned home after walking the distance. The dog's name was Butch and he became my father's favourite after that. My father had a very soft side to him, especially with animals.

The father I loved spent time with me and made things with wood. He once made a doll-size wooden replica of our house with the exact same rooms and windows. The roof lifted off so we could put our dolls inside. It was the best dolls house I ever saw and I played with it often.

My father drove a bread truck, delivering bread to the small corner shops before their opening time. During school holidays, he would take me on his delivery run. I looked forward to that immensely, and although I had to get up very early, it made me feel special to be at work with my father. Every shopkeeper on his delivery list made us sit down and eat something while my father amused them with his new Irish jokes. My father loved his mouth organ and sometimes sat on his bed playing it. He loved our above ground swimming pool. Sometimes on hot summer days, I would find him alone in the pool floating on a rubber tyre. He always wore a large brimmed hat.

The man I feared drank to excess on most days and spent much of the family budget on alcohol. My father often smelt of alcohol, but he would deny that he had been drinking. He would hide the bottles in the garbage bin under all the rubbish. When he drank too much he became argumentative, aggressive, and sometimes violent towards my mother or whoever stood in the way. He would sometimes argue and verbally abuse me. After arguing with my mother, he would reject us by going quiet and staying in his room. He would not speak to anyone in the house for sometimes weeks. During these times, I felt alone and unwanted by my father. I believed it was me who had done something wrong and that is why he did not talk to me.

My father was very secretive about his drinking and used to get his money for alcohol from the local pawn shop. He would pawn something he did not think my mother would miss. One day, the iron went missing, which caused a bit of a problem. I wondered why he might have thought we would not miss the iron.

My father seemed to cruise through parenthood with little interest in how we were clothed, fed, and mentored, but he was happy to laugh and play. He had no interest in our schooling or homework. Whenever I would go to my father to ask him for something, my father always replied, 'Ask your mother'.

My mother was born in England in the early 1930s. She was an only child, and she often told us stories of a cruel childhood, where she suffered much abuse from her mother and father. She liked to sew and loved the garden. I remember she was always doing many different jobs and she seemed good at whatever she did. My mother had a good sense of humour and made me laugh a lot.

My mother was also two women to me. One that loved and cared for me, and another that was distant and unattached, which made me also fearful of her. My mother worked very hard and often long hours due to the travel involved. We had very little money to show for the hours of work my mother put in.

Even though she worked and travelled for long hours, she was there for me when I needed a cuddle. I remember a time when I went to her in tears and she talked to me and gave me a hug. She often told me she loved me. She looked after me whenever I was sick and she made healthy food, especially for those times. My mother tried her hardest to pay for me to go on school excursions or buy me some clothes when I needed them. She had a soft side to her, and I believe she had a desire to give us what she never had as a child. I remember when I was learning about religion at school, and I talked about it a lot. My mother presented me with a beautiful statue of Jesus that she had saved hard to buy. I can recall her joy when she presented it to me. My mother taught me to sew and to drive a car.

The mother that I feared had unpredictable outbursts of aggression. I liken my mother to a kitchen appliance we had at home whilst I was growing up. It was called a pressure cooker. The cooker sat on the gas stove top and looked like a large saucepan with a tight-fitting lid. There was a little hat shaped metal valve on the lid. When the temperature inside the saucepan started to rise, the valve would start to wobble like mad. Then small amounts of steam would be released in order to keep a constant temperature inside the saucepan. When the cooking time was reached, the steam would shoot up around the valve as it wobbled uncontrollably and made a whistling sound. The noise was to alert you to the rising pressure and the impending escape of hot steam. When that happened, my mother would take it off the stove or turn the heat down.

I can liken the tension in the house sometimes to a pressure cooker. My mother rarely said a bad word that I could remember but internally, her emotions would brew and brew. The pressure inside her would start to rise and then all of a sudden *bang*! She would explode in a rage and we would all run for cover, sometimes not even knowing what her rage was about or who it was aimed at. During her rage, anything was likely to come out of her mouth and sometimes it was very hurtful to whoever her rage was directed.

Whilst I was young, I did not have the maturity to recognise any warning signs of the rising pressure and therefore had very few places to hide when she erupted. As I got older, it became easier for me to predict when her valve was going to explode. I could then recognise the right time to leave the house or go to the confines of my bedroom.

I remember the struggles we had with money. On several occasions, we had the gas and electricity disconnected because the bills went unpaid.

When we had no electricity, my father cooked our dinner on a metal plate, which he placed over a wooden fire at the rear of the garden. We had cold showers and lived by candlelight until there was enough money for reconnection. I hated trips to the supermarket because when we got to the check out with our groceries, my mother often did not have enough money. This meant that we had to put several items back. Choosing the items was often difficult because they formed part of the ingredients needed for one of our meals. I disliked shopping for that reason because it would be my job to put the items back on the shelves. I found that embarrassing.

I can also remember a black leather lounge that had been bought under a loan arrangement. It came into the house and only a short time later, it went out the door again after being repossessed. This happened to several of our cars, televisions, and other furniture. Whenever I saw a truck arrive out the front of our house, I knew that someone was coming to take something away from us.

At one time, we had a television that was rented. It had a coin box connected to the back of it. When we wanted to watch television, my mother used to put a twenty cent coin in the coin box. After the required amount of time, the coin would drop and the television screen would go black. We scrounged around for more coins as quick as we could so we did not miss too much of our favourite show.

CHAPTER 4

SHATTERED MEMORIES—
THE TRAUMA OF DOMESTIC VIOLENCE

> You won't miraculously become happy if someone else changes, or if the outside world changes, but only if you change.
>
> (Brian L. Weiss)

In amongst the difficulties of raising five children, my parent's relationship was volatile. As I got older, I started to become aware of some loud arguments between my mother and father. I first recall hearing them when I was in third class at school at around the age of eight or nine.

The atmosphere in our house was sometimes tense and we all knew that meant an argument was brewing. Whenever my brothers and sisters were around, it was safety in numbers with the five of us in the house. I felt safer when my brothers were at home because they would sometimes stand up to my father.

My father and grandmother's relationship was also volatile and they disliked each other, immensely. My grandmother often interfered when my mother and father were arguing, and she would defend my mother and denigrate my father. It often became my mother and grandmother against my father. This made my father very frustrated and made me feel sorry for my father.

I recall a time when my mother told me that she was taking us to Brisbane to live, and my father would not be coming with us. I had little understanding of what was going on but I remember worrying about my father being left behind. I loved my father and I did not want to leave him on his own.

In the days before the train trip to Brisbane, I had to say goodbye to my school friends and my teacher. I think I was about eight years old when I packed up all the belongings in my desk and I left. I remember the confusion and lack of understanding, which I felt at the time because I was not only leaving my friends but my home and my father. The two most secure parts of my childhood were changing but I had no choice in the matter. It was natural for my friends to be curious and ask questions, but I did not have the answers. I pretended to be excited because I did not want my friends to see me sad. I remember feeling sad, but I also felt it was an adventure as well. We packed up our belongings and my mother, grandmother, and the five of us boarded the train headed for Brisbane. The trip took about fourteen hours. We played board games whilst my younger sister slept on the floor under the table. When we got to Brisbane, we stayed in a hotel where I remember the beds had starched white sheets. I was scared sleeping in the hotel room because it was dark and unfamiliar. When I needed to go to the toilet in the middle of the night, I was too frightened to move and ended up accidentally wetting the bed.

Our visit to Brisbane was short-lived and after only one or two nights my mother put us all back on the train again and we returned home. When we arrived back to our house in St Marys, my father was there and I was so happy to see him. He looked very sad and did not say much to us. The house was the same, but my father had moved all the furniture from every room of our house into the front lounge room. I thought that was a bit weird. I guess it gave my father something to do.

A few days after saying goodbye to my school, I found myself returning to the same classroom, same desk, and the same teacher. The children kept asking me why I was back at school and in an attempt to ignore the questions and their teasing; I would just say 'My mum changed her mind'.

I remember being the subject of a lot of teasing for some time after my return. I did not really understand why, but I think the children just picked on someone that was outside the norm. The trip to Brisbane made me feel different to the other kids. That just matched in with my freckles.

CHAPTER 5

RAW FEAR—A SCARRED CHILD

> I was an innocent child frozen with fear, not knowing what to do for those who were meant to protect me, were the cause of my fear. I return as an adult, to take the hand of that child. I will lead you to safety and you need not feel fear, no more.
>
> (Sharon Gardiner)

Sometime after our Brisbane trip, I can vividly recall a day in my childhood where my mother and father started to argue loudly and aggressively. When they did argue, their voices got so loud they ended up shouting at each other. The shouting seemed to go on for a long time and I became frightened.

This day, I just wanted the arguing to stop because it seemed like it took over our whole house and bellowed into the neighbourhood as well. My two brothers would have normally protected us but they weren't home this day. I remember, my older sister was there and I think she might have been aged around fourteen at the time.

She was pleading with my mother and father to calm down and wanting them to stop. The argument just got worse and the shouting was getting louder and louder. I heard my sister continue to try to calm my parents down, but nothing she said made them stop. My sister was being very brave, but I was so unbelievably scared that day. I went into the corner of the dining room and cowered behind the dining room table. I buried my face into my hands whilst I huddled in the corner as if I was trying to warm myself during a freezing blizzard. I tried to be invisible. My mother and father were in the hallway opposite their bedroom door. As their yelling got louder and more aggressive, I screamed louder and cried more. I was petrified with fear. My father was yelling something about my mother and another man and then I heard a thud and my mother started to cry, saying something about her nose.

The shouting and banging noise of my father's fists hitting the wall seemed to continue for such a long time that it felt like, time stood still. I heard my sister on the phone talking to the police. While we waited for the police to arrive, she continued to plead with my parents to stop and then she would turn to me and tell me that it was going to be OK.

It seemed a long time before I heard a knock at the front door and my sister went to answer it. Then I saw a policeman walk past me, heading towards the hallway. I don't know if he saw me, but I am sure he heard me crying. I noticed he was dressed smartly in his uniform and soon after his arrival, the shouting stopped. I stayed huddled under the table in the corner of the room and I was sobbing, uncontrollably and still too scared to move. The policeman took my father outside. When they both returned, the policeman stood and looked at me. I heard him speak to my sister.

He said 'Is she OK?' (referring to me)

My sister replied, 'Yeah, she is OK, I'll look after her.'

The policeman left and I can clearly remember thinking that I did not want him to leave, without taking me with him. I was so scared I did not know what to do.

'What is a child meant to do in that situation?'

I felt helpless and so scared. I was supposed to be protected by my parents and not be huddled in the corner so scared because of them. If I focused on my memory of that day long enough, I can feel a shiver up my spine. I have never felt so terrified at any other time in my life. I can still picture in my mind the policeman's face when he looked at me as I cowered in the corner.

I was living in the grips of a volatile situation, where any rising pressure or tension could cause a blow up. The situation I found myself in that day was terrible and the impact of that day has become cemented in my memory. I saw that police officer like my knight in shining armour because he stopped the shouting and argument at least for that day anyway!

My father was a strange character after the arguments. He would just go quiet and not speak to anyone in our house, for sometimes, weeks or months. During this time of silence, I felt alone and rejected. It was an unfair rejection of us during our childhood, but I guess it was my father's way of manipulating and controlling the situation. My mother supported us and tried to act normal. She would tell us that it was not something that we had done to cause my father to ignore us, but I did not really understand that. I missed my father during that time.

I remember touching the bridge of my mother's nose, and I could feel a gap in the bone that was not meant to be there. My mother always put on a brave face even though she must have been terribly distressed. I could not relate to the pain that my mother must have felt that day, but I can relate to an intense feeling of fear that she too might have experienced.

CHAPTER 6

AN ERA OF MISGUIDED DISCIPLINE—
SOCIETY GOT IT WRONG

Children are meant to be seen and not heard.

(Unknown)

In the 1970s, I think discipline was regarded as a deterrent to keep children well behaved and out of trouble. Whatever means of discipline the parents chose appeared to be accepted and almost encouraged by some parts of society. Discipline was dished out not only in the home but at school as well. Each household seemed to have their own ideas of discipline. What comes to my mind is a lashing with the trouser belt, soap spread over the tongue (for swearing or backchat), or a wooden spoon slapped around the legs or on the hand. My grandmother often said that children were meant to be seen and not heard.

In my own experience, the verbal abuse that I witnessed and endured as a child far outweighed, having soap spread over my tongue. The soap just tasted bitter and could be washed away. The verbal abuse would cut deep emotionally, and the scars could last my life time.

I felt I was brought up more as a possession with no right to question my parent's decisions. Not being able to question my parents left me with a lack of understanding of the reasoning behind their actions and therefore

I could easily perceive something as being my fault in some way. I was not game to question my parents out of fear of repercussions.

I had a similar experience at school when I remember receiving some punishments as a child in year four. This happened on at least three separate occasions. As punishment for not handing in my homework, I was caned by my year four teacher Mr T with the handle of the feather duster. Mr T did not believe me when I told him another student had taken my homework. I could see my homework sitting under the other student's desk. He only needed to spend the time to listen to my side of the story, but instead, I was taken into the storeroom and told to hold out my hand. Mr T then hit my hand three times with the handle of the feather duster. I don't recall it hurting that much physically, but I was again humiliated amongst my peers.

Whilst I was growing up, my mother constantly reminded me of the mistakes she had made in her younger years. I believe that she was determined to instil into my brain the importance of making something out of my life. She often talked to me about teenage pregnancy and to my brothers about drugs, alcohol, and crime. I listened to her intently when I was by myself, but I also listened again whilst she told the same story to my brothers and sisters as well. I was so scared that I might make the mistake of getting pregnant. I asked my mother if I could go on the contraceptive pill. This was before I had really even thought about having sex. I think I was more scared of her reaction and disappointment if I did get pregnant than actually getting pregnant.

It was clear to me from an early age that she wanted better for us than what she was able to give us and also accomplish in her own life. I took that to heart every time she reminded us and it became my mission to achieve as much as possible in life. In return for my achievements, I expected to be rewarded with her pride, acceptance, and approval. After all I believed I was doing what she wanted.

The difficulty for me during my childhood years was that I observed my parent's volatile relationship and their individual struggles to find themselves, in amongst all of it. Their relationship was certainly not a positive one and not the sought of relationship one would want to model or imitate as an adult. I saw my parents treating each other appallingly. The verbal abuse was not just limited to between them but me and my brothers and sisters as well. The verbal abuse was really not that constructive and necessary for discipline but intended to be hurtful instead. I believe the verbal abuse was used more to satisfy my parent's own needs. I think I would be correct if I said the verbal abuse was really to make themselves feel better, by propping up their own poor self-worth.

Even in those years of volatility, my mother still had the wisdom and strength to attempt to change the fate of her own children. I can't speak for my brothers and sisters, but for me I took those words of wisdom and made success my mission in life.

By this stage in my life, my programming had begun. The once beautiful precious pearl accepted by all at birth had received many conflicting messages. It was these messages and my own perception of them that were beginning to determine my path from childhood to an adult.

CHAPTER 7

MY MOTHER'S MESSAGES—
INCONSISTENCY AND CONFUSION

> You cannot learn other people's lessons for them. They must do the work themselves, and they'll do it when they are ready.
>
> (Louise L. Hay)

My mother had instilled in me, the ideal that I should never treat anyone any different to how I would want to be treated myself.

This was a message with two meanings for me. On one hand, be nice to everyone and on the other hand, let them abuse you both emotionally and physically. I heard one message constantly but saw my mother acting differently, nearly every other day.

'Did she think that it was acceptable for my father to treat her in that manner?' I don't believe so.

Or 'did she believe that she herself was not worthy of being treated with any level of respect?'

I was confused by these mixed messages and lacked understanding of what I was actually meant to be doing. I think from a child's perspective, mixed messages can lead to confusion and therefore misrepresentation of that message.

In amongst my father's abuse towards my mother, I would sometimes hear my mother verbally abuse my brother and sister. I heard her yelling at them one day and saying things like; they were good for nothing, fat dole bludgers. She would follow that up with comments like get your fat arses out of the house and get a job, or you be out on the street. I felt humiliated for them, and believed my mother to be cruel with her words. My sister started to cry and I felt so sad for her because my mother's words were so mean and hurtful.

It was not long before it was my time to experience my mother's pressure cooker moment and my own humiliation. I remember a time in my late school years when I started to go out with a nice boy. We got on well together and loved to chat. One night he came over to my house. We wanted to have some privacy away from my family, so we sat in the front seat of his car, which was parked in front of our house. We just wanted to hang out together and talk about stuff that teenagers normally did. Before we knew it, we had talked all night and the sun had started to come up. I think we might have dozed for some periods but all we did was talk and maybe, hold each other's hand. I thought it was pretty innocent. As the sun was rising and the birds started to sing, I heard the front screen door open and close with a familiar bang. I looked up to see my mother come marching out of the house towards us. I was old enough now to be able to recognise the signs that the wobbly pressure cooker valve was about to rupture. At that moment, she started yelling at me to get out of the car and then she yelled 'What will the neighbours think?'

The next words from her mouth were some pretty harsh and demoralising ones. She spoke with the presumption that I had had sex with this boy in the car for all to see. I was so embarrassed and humiliated for both of us that I cried and then just wanted to hide under the nearest rock. I felt so small and insignificant. I had not done anything wrong with this boy, but instead had really enjoyed, just being able to talk to him all night long about anything. I was really disappointed that my mother could even think that about me, and it became obvious that she did not trust me. I was disappointed in her, not only for the humiliation she caused, but the fact that she also must have thought I did not listen to her advice.

I had always been a fairly private person, prior to that incident, but after that, I kept what I got up to, very close to my chest indeed. Her chastising did not teach me any lessons other than to go underground and hide what I was up to. In looking back, I think I formed the opinion that it did not really matter what I did because my mother obviously thought little of me. I believe I rebelled after that incident because I felt angry that she could think such a thing about me. I can still feel the humiliation of that morning. I bet that nice young boy can to.

'Can you relate to a similar time when you were chastised in front of your peers for something that was significant to you?'

I believe we all can.

'Can you see a pattern that may have brought you to this point, where your self-esteem or feeling of self-worth may be in need of repair, well into adulthood?'

These were the type of mixed messages I received on a daily basis and I am sure my brothers and sisters heard their own mixed messages.

On another occasion, I found myself both the cause and recipient of one of my mother's pressure cooker moments.

As a newly licensed driver, I had been driving around the local area for hours without telling my mother where I was (no mobile phones in those days). When I got home, I realised she was sick with worry and that came out in a burst of anger, frustration, and aggression. She yelled and screamed her disappointment and then got stuck into me with the hairbrush, hitting me very hard several times around the head in a complete rage. She was out of control so my brother intervened and rescued me before she did any physical damage but the emotional damage, just added to my already damaged state. I can laugh looking back at that time because the hairbrush was made by the cosmetic company 'Avon'. It was white with black bristles. That hairbrush lasted for years and years afterward. Every time I shop for a new hairbrush, I aim to find one as sturdy as that one.

I felt for my mother when she got so angry and went into her rages. She was obviously stressed and frustrated. That wasn't that difficult for me to figure out even from an early age.

I wanted to try and help my mother as much as I could. The main reason was for my own survival because I did not want to be treated in the same way that I had heard my brother and sister being treated. I also wanted to avoid being the recipient of more of her pressure cooker moments.

I decided that I needed to be as independent as I possibly could. I loved my mother and recognised that it was hard for her. She always talked about the amount of work she had to do. On her days off, she felt she had to spend her time cleaning instead of relaxing. I was old enough to know that if she could not get some relaxing time then this would add to her stress, which might increase the possibility of more pressure cooker moments.

I definitely wanted to avoid this, so on Saturday mornings whilst my mother and older sister were out shopping; I started to clean the house. I attempted to help her so she had less to do. I wanted to be more helpful around the house, less dependent and as a result of that, nearly invisible. In return I thought I could avoid any trouble.

I took my desire to be independent to the extreme and went out and got my first job at Coles Supermarket working Thursday evening and Saturday mornings. I worked a second job at the restaurant my mother managed called Happy Grannys. I was attending school Monday to Friday, working my first job Thursday evening and Saturday morning and then at the restaurant most of the weekend including some Friday nights. I was raking in good money for someone so young, but as a consequence of that, I was doing very little of my school work.

I loved to sew and therefore made my own senior school uniforms. You name it, I tried to do it. I was on a mission to help my mother as much as I could and the harder I worked, I believed the less chance I had of coming under her notice. I wanted to be as far from the limelight as possible. I was determined to avoid the same humiliation that I felt my brother and sister had endured. At the same time, I wanted my mother to be pleased with what I was doing to help her but most of all, I wanted her approval.

CHAPTER 8

INDEPENDENCE—HIDING UNDER THE RADAR

An Investment in knowledge pays the best interest.

(Ben Franklin)

In the midst of all my independence, I was called into the Principal's office after a miserable end of year eleven report. I don't recall my mother or father attending that meeting but that was not unusual. My father never participated in our school life. I don't know if my father even knew where the school was located and my mother was usually working or too tired. I can recall a time during my school years when I had a solo role in a school play as Julius Caesar. I stood on the stage in front of everyone else's parents because my mother said she was too tired to come. My father dropped me off at the concert and picked me up afterward.

The Principal of my school was a lovely man whom I respected, and I felt he was one of the first adults that actually listened to what I had to say. He told me that he believed I was a very capable student. He commented that I was not working to my potential and I should think about whether I should continue on to year twelve to complete my higher school certificate.

I considered what we had discussed and thought carefully about returning to school. I spoke to my main teachers, whom I also respected, and as a result I did return to year twelve as scheduled. I only lasted until about the second term and therefore did not complete my final year of high school.

I look back now and realise that I made my decision so flippantly with little understanding of the consequences to my future and little guidance from my parents. My mother left the decision in my hands and my father would have just said, 'Ask your mother'.

This meant that the decision was up to me and considering I was only seventeen at the time, I made the choice to leave. It was when I saw my friend's graduate that I knew my decision was the wrong one and something that I would live to regret. I believe education is so important for many reasons but mostly for your own progression in life. I just did not have that insight when I had only just turned seventeen.

Regardless of my decision, I was determined to make something out of my life and therefore started working full-time as a canteen assistant at the Sydney Opera House. After a short time there, I had enough money to move out of home with my brother and rent a unit in a Sydney suburb called Neutral Bay. I was still only seventeen at the time, but this was a great opportunity to move away from home. I wanted more independence, but most of all, I wanted to get out and live life to the fullest without suffering the effects of my mother's disapproval. I felt my mother had formed an opinion of me that disappointed her in some way so I wanted to experience life without worrying about what she thought.

CHAPTER 9

LOOKING FOR LOVE—IN ALL THE WRONG PLACES

> Everything in your life . . . every experience, every relationship . . .
> is a mirror of the mental pattern that's going on inside you.
>
> (Louise L. Hay)

I had left home as a young adolescent, and it was not long after that when I can recall feeling that there was something missing in my life. Around that age, I don't believe I had the insight or understanding of what exactly that missing part of me might have been. I was no longer within the confines of home and school but living in an adult world. I had different people around me, and this created the opportunity for me to be influenced by different peer groups. I essentially just drifted along and did what I thought was good at the time.

It was as I started to get older and gain some life experience that I started to really think about what it was that I was missing. These thoughts led me to reflect on the relationships I developed during my childhood and adolescence. I believed the most significant relationship that I had throughout childhood was the one with my mother and father. What I think was most important for me to receive out of that relationship was unconditional love, approval, and acceptance. That is all I really wanted. I needed to feel like I was loved for who I was as a person. I did not feel that I could get what I needed from my mother and father, so I started to look elsewhere.

I was seventeen when my brother (2nd oldest) and I moved in together into Neutral Bay. I was working full-time and earning good money so it seemed like the perfect chance to move away from home. As children, my brother and I had some fun times growing up and we got on well together. We were close as brother and sister, but we also had our own interests as well.

We were similar in a lot of ways with the same fair complexion, hair colour, and our bodies covered in freckles. We both enjoyed a good laugh and had sensitive, caring natures. We were easy-going, enjoyed each other's company, and looked after each other as best we knew how.

Our living arrangement was so different to what we had both been used to whilst growing up, it was predictable, respectful, and we were both equally important within the household.

Although our experiences were different, we both lived to some degree in the shadow of our childhood influences. We wanted different things in life, but we had the common struggle of overcoming a feeling of self loathing or not feeling good enough. This struggle connected us together even more.

My brother rode a motorcycle and when he went out at night, I used to worry about him getting home safe. If he had a late night out, I would sleep lightly until I heard his bike come down the driveway. When he arrived home, I could relax and drift off to sleep soundly.

I have fond memories of that time because I felt that I had someone to care for and someone cared for me. I had a great sense of family with both my brothers and I felt very special, being able to live with one of them. We cared for each other so much.

One afternoon I came home a little worse for wear. I had gone horse riding with a friend and had a rather spectacular fall onto the hard ground. Initially, I lost all feeling in my body, and I had a moment where I thought I was not going to be able to walk again, but thank goodness it was not lasting.

I managed somehow to get myself back on the horse and then later return home on the train. I remember walking up the hundreds of stairs at Wynyard underground railway station in the Sydney CBD. I was in so much pain I had to take one step at a time, hanging on to the handrail as I took each step upward. I saw a grey-haired lady with a walking stick overtaking me. I must have been a sorry sight because she stopped and asked me if I needed help.

She said in such a caring manner, 'You poor thing, dear, can I help you?'

I declined her assistance because I just wanted to take my time with every step and I was a bit embarrassed. I watched her figure disappear as she seemed to manage the stairs at lightning speed compared to me. I eventually got home and because I was in so much pain, my brother took me to the local hospital. I was relieved when the doctor told me my pain was caused by just bad bruising. I looked like I had laid on a blue ink pad because it went from my bra strap to both buttocks. I could walk but found it painful to stand for too long.

I loved my job and wanted to go to work every day, but it was going to prove challenging due to my inability to move freely. Getting in and out of bed was the worst part. For about two weeks, my brother got up earlier every morning to help me out of bed and every night he helped me get back. This went on for about two weeks and I could not have got through it without his help.

I felt that what my brother and I had together was what a real family meant. My brother looked out for me and I looked out for him but most of all we had respect for each other.

I recall another time when I went out on my first date with one of his friends. It was a double date with my brother and his girlfriend at the time. The date ended when we were saying our goodbyes with a kiss. That was when I felt his tongue thrust down my throat. I was shocked because I had never experienced that before and I thought it was disgusting. Maybe if I had had some warning, I would not have been so disgusted. I told my brother what had happened and we spent the whole afternoon in absolute hysterics, laughing uncontrollably. The moments that we laughed together were very special.

My brother was very protective of me and the first time I brought a male home to stay overnight, he got annoyed with me. This resulted in a lecture about one-night stands, casual sex, and not giving myself away to quick. He was pretty tough on me, but I appreciated his concern. Looking back, I wished he would have explained what he was trying to say in more detail because I did not totally understand, what he meant. At the time I listened to my brother more than anyone.

In those few words that he did say, I think he was really talking about having respect for myself. When I think about what respect meant to me then, I think of what my mother had said about treating others in a manner that you would want to be treated yourself. I perceived respect as being nice to people and not hurt them in anyway, either physically or emotionally. This was in stark contrast to what I had seen growing up, so I was confused. I didn't feel I was worthy of the same respect and I couldn't explain why.

The importance of how the other person felt distracted me from worrying too much about what was best for me.

I disliked what I saw of myself in the mirror and was very critical of the way I looked and was seen by others. As a young girl, I don't remember anyone talking about the term self-esteem. I think as girls at school, we talked mostly about what we didn't like about ourselves and in particular, our bodies. The notion of poor self-image or esteem was evident to us, but I don't remember it being discussed as openly to the degree it is today. I don't believe we associated, talking about the things we disliked about ourselves as a bad thing. The concept of not liking yourself seemed innocuous and therefore lacked importance to me at the time. This is a different story in my later years when I realised the magnitude of a poor self worth and the impact it can have on the way I lived my life.

Whilst I considered myself as being young and not so worldly at seventeen, I was in the workforce fulltime, living away from home with a smorgasbord of men around me. I found this an exciting time. I wanted to enjoy my freedom and independence without the risk of being humiliated or judged.

Looking back, I think my brother knew me better than I knew myself and he was right when he talked about self-respect. I didn't feel driven by self-respect. I felt driven by the need to find love, affection, and approval in a world where I felt, there was little acceptance of who I was. I started to date lots of different men and no matter what sort of date it was, it always ended in sex at some point. I craved the affection most of all because it made me feel wanted and loved, even though it was momentary or short-lived.

I met a few men that I dated for a period of time, but when I felt like I was no longer getting love, affection, and approval, I would move on to the next. The passion of a new partner was so much more exciting for me because the level of affection was high.

In my early years, I had started to drink alcohol to excess. This caused some problems for me because I was frequently invited to parties within my workplace. My work colleagues kept a close eye on me in most cases because they cared for me, but it was also up to me to be a bit responsible.

I was living in a grown-up world, but I was still only a child in a lot of ways. I was lucky to have some older mentors around me that would talk to me and give me a bit of guidance. I did listen to them because they always spoke to me in a respectful way. I continued with a few longer-term relationships and I started to settle down in relation to dating. I did not look at most of my acquaintances as lasting because I always seemed to be treated poorly. I don't mean emotionally or physically, I mean treated with lack of respect, never answering my calls, cancelling dates at the last minute. I put up with these males because I got, what I thought was love, affection, and approval. I recognised that there was something not right about what I was doing in relation to dating but I had little insight or maturity as to what it was.

There were times when I did stand up for myself and speak out. One particular male I was with for over six months. He seemed nice until I declined to smoke 'pot' with five of his friends. I was not into pot, smoking or drugs of any kind. I grew up in a smoke-filled house, where the yellow nicotine ran down the walls when the kitchen steamed up, after cooking. I was not going to pollute my already passive-smoked lungs for any amount of love, affection, or approval. I proudly ditched that bloke and not long after, I heard that he had made his way into prison for dealing drugs.

I realised then that I was capable of making some pretty good decisions although infrequently. I had set some standards for myself even amongst the lack of self-respect. When my standards were challenged, I could speak out . . . how weird!

CHAPTER 10

BOOZE, SEX, AND BARELY SEVENTEEN— LIKE A BULL IN A CHINA SHOP

> It ain't where you start, it's where you end up that counts
>
> Author unknown.

I was still only seventeen, but I had access to as much alcohol as I wanted. It was no surprise that I couldn't handle the amount of alcohol I was drinking because I was just too young to be even drinking it. The barman where I worked took the time to sit me down and talk to me about my choice of alcoholic drinks. He was another whom I respected and I listened to his advice intently. I drank Bacardi and coke, but he suggested I changed to Bacardi and orange juice instead. It did seem to make a difference for me or maybe it was the fact that I was becoming more aware of the effect too much alcohol had on me.

I was the youngest one in my workplace and I likened myself to a bull in a china shop out to experience life with little regard for consequences. There were always plenty of in house work functions to attend throughout the year but particularly during the time leading up to Christmas. I felt safe within this environment and my home life was also safe, so life was good for me at that time.

One night, I attended a Christmas party, outside the normal range of parties that I usually attended. This particular party was for a group of men that I had little to do with, but I saw them every day. I decided to go to their party with another female work colleague. When I got there, I started to drink and had my usual dose of alcohol.

I was asked by one of the men if I would like to see the backstage area. I knew this man, and I trusted him because he was married with children. I was curious to see what was behind the many doors so I went with him. I had no idea where I was being taken because it was dark and after normal working hours. We ended up in a room that was very dark and secluded. We had walked through quite a few sound doors to get there. The room had this eerie silence to it and I felt disorientated due to the darkness.

Soon after we got there, he started to kiss me, and I initially reciprocated but I felt pretty uncomfortable, so I stopped. He was unattractive to me, many years older and very obese with a hard beer gut that poked out at the bottom of his T-shirt. He had dark hair with a bushy beard.

I started to question where he had taken me and then I became suspicious of his intentions. I did not think that anything would happen because I trusted him, but I soon realised he had brought me to the place with the intention of having sex. I did not want his attention.

It was then that his hands started to touch me in places that made me feel uncomfortable. He touched my breasts and crotch and I kept moving his hands away. He persisted and I started telling him to stop.

The thought of having sex with him just made me feel disgusting, even in my inebriated state, so I was determined to refuse. I had no idea where I was or even where to find the door.

He was tall and very strong and it was so dark with no lights. He kept trying to kiss me and then his hands started to grab me, firmly. It was not long before I ended up on the ground with his heavy body on top of me. I kept telling him I did not want to have sex but I knew that I was not going to be able to get myself out of this situation. I felt his erect penis pushing up against my leg and the weight of his large firm gut, pushing me into the floor. I had no way of overpowering him. I felt my clothing being pulled off, including my underwear. I don't remember much about the sex other than the rhythmic thrusts of his huge hard gut hitting my stomach. I felt his body hair on my bare skin.

I repeated my plea to stop but he just kept going. I did not fight, I did not struggle. I just kept thinking that I had done the wrong thing coming to this dark place with him, drinking too much and trusting him. I felt that I got myself into that situation, so it was my fault. I felt I was to blame not him, and I felt ashamed. I blocked out what was going on as a way of just coping until he stopped. The whole thing happened so quickly, but felt to me like it would never end. I got dressed and spoke very little to him whilst we made our way back through the dark corridors. He took me back to the party. I stayed silent and on return to the party, I spoke to no one. I went home as quickly as I could.

Three nights later, I was talking to one of my regular male friends and I told him only parts of what had happened because I felt so ashamed. I believed it was my fault and that is why I have never disclosed that story to anyone. The reason I am telling my story in my book, some thirty-five years later, is because I can look back on that incident and see it for what it was. At the time, I thought I was the one to blame because I contributed to making it happen, therefore I believed I deserved what happened. It was not till later in life that I saw the incident for what it was and that is sexual assault.

I can't explain exactly why I decided not to tell anyone about that incident. I felt embarrassed, ashamed, and guilty. I blamed myself; after all I blamed myself for most of the things that happened in life even when I had little to do with them. I was accustomed to blaming myself.

After that night, I started to rethink my behaviour and certainly tone down my alcohol intake. I learnt from that experience not to be so trusting but never the less, I was still in need of love, affection, and approval and the need became similar to an addiction.

CHAPTER 11

EMOTIONAL WOUNDS NEED HEALING TOO— A NURTURING PROFESSION

> Nobody really ever knows, how much anybody else, is hurting. We could be standing next to somebody who is, completely broken and we wouldn't even know.
>
> (Unknown)

Whilst I was working at the Opera House, I applied to start a nursing career which was something I always wanted to do. My first hospital of choice was Royal North Shore because it was a large distinguished place. The building towered over the grass fields that separated it from the Pacific Highway and therefore looked enchanting to me. My mother also worked there for some years so I was familiar with it. I felt lucky to get an interview, but I was swiftly told that because my parents were common labourers from the western suburbs of Sydney I would not be offered a position. I was also told that they only took on the children of doctors, lawyers, and business owners. They also scathed at the fact, I did not have my higher school certificate. Employers did not have the same workplace regulations (in 1977) as we do have today, and I don't believe discrimination in the workplace was on the agenda back then. I just took what they said as reality and that I was not worthy of employment so I looked elsewhere.

I was determined to find a hospital that would take me. I kept trying and was accepted into a small city hospital who did not even ask about my parents. It was April 1979 when I moved away from my brother and into the nurse's home at Balmain District Hospital.

During my nurses training, I formed some great friendships that taught me so much about life and relationships. On arrival at the nurse's home, I shared a room with a girl from the country who was so scared of being in the city. We formed a close and enjoyable friendship. She loved the simple things in life and was dedicated to her study. I could never get higher marks than her, but it was fun trying. We also met another girl and the three of us became good friends throughout our training days. They both taught me so much about friendship and family. I look back on our friendship with heartfelt pleasure.

I also met my long-term friend Deborah when she was a senior nurse on a surgical ward.

We soon became best friends and moved in together in a house at Rozelle, just up from the famous, Rose Shamrock and Thistle Pub, better known as 'The Three Weeds'.

She taught me about love, tolerance, and respect for each other as well as the importance of doing what is right for you. I watched as the relationship with her boyfriend Greg (now husband) grew, and I admired the love they had for each other. They did everything from one united point where each person's opinion or ideals were as important as each other. It was a stable relationship and one I had not witnessed before.

Deborah attempted to guide me with my own relationships and I did listen, but I still needed to continue in my search for love and affection. She moved on at the completion of her training but we had formed a long time, lasting friendship. I then moved in with another friend named

Kim and two other nurses. We lived above the pet shop in the main street of Balmain.

I met Kim on our first day of nursing when our class got together. She liked to laugh a lot and this attracted me to her. Kim was a carefree type of person but at the same time headstrong and ambitious. She was a loyal friend, non-judgemental, light-hearted, and caring. She lived life to the fullest and never knocked back an opportunity for any new experience.

I remember the days, she spent in her room, and I would sit on the side of her bed and just chat about girl stuff. She used to talk to me, about the right ways that people should treat each other and would tell me to get rid of the guys that did not live up to that standard. I felt so much a part of something special with her and that was so important to me. I thought our friendship was wonderful and she was someone I could confide in at any time.

When we both finished our training, we kept in close contact. I began working in a larger hospital and moved to their onsite accommodation. It was the Friday of the October long weekend in 1983 when I waved her goodbye as she left for a three day break with her boyfriend. I told her to have a great time and take care. I watched them ride off into the distance.

During that weekend, I was shocked to hear the news that Kim had died tragically whilst a pillion passenger on her boyfriend's motorcycle. I remember the day vividly. It was about 2.15 p.m. when I was getting dressed to go to work for an afternoon shift starting at 3 p.m. until 11.30 p.m. I heard the phone ringing but I was running out of time to get ready, so I did not answer it. The phone rang a second time so I reluctantly answered it. I heard my mother's voice. Her voice was shaky and she was speaking with some hesitancy. My mind was focused on getting ready for work when

I heard my mother say, 'Kim is dead'.

I did not believe what I was hearing and I started to cry.

It appeared that they had come over a crest and straight into the bull bar of another vehicle. She was killed instantly on impact at the age of twenty-two. I was shocked.

My flatmate at the time consoled me and informed work that I would be late. I felt I had no choice other than to go to work because of the time. When I got there, amongst my colleagues and friends, I broke down in despair and was clearly unable to work. One of my friends (Cathy) drove me home to be with my family. My mother and brother consoled me that day but unbeknown to me, my experience of grief and loss was about to hit me like a tornado.

Kim's funeral was one of the saddest days I can remember. I was in disbelief, lost my direction in life and without her I felt so alone. I missed her terribly. I did not attend her viewing prior to the funeral because I was accidentally not informed about it. I regretted that I did not have a chance to say goodbye to her and that added to my sadness. I was lucky to have been out with her the night prior to her riding into the distance so I hung on to that memory.

At the time of Kim's death, I was working in an area of nursing that was very taxing emotionally. It was a neurosurgical ward full of tragedy. The ward was occupied with a large proportion of young people who had sustained brain injury as a result of road trauma or some form of assault. These patients could stay on the ward for as long as nine months. During this time the patient, their relatives, and the staff became like one close knit family.

It was an emotionally intense area with constant highs and lows. The staff on the ward were remarkable and the camaraderie exceptional. I was a person who gave everything of myself to my patients, relatives, and colleagues. There were many of us like that, and we became an extended family for the relatives and patients of the ward. It was a ward that was full of happiness one minute when an unconscious patient would wake up and speak their first word or in stark contrast terrible sadness when another patient might take their last breath. The nurses were there for the families as they needed us, but we were also there for each other.

In amongst the emotional highs and lows of the ward, I was experiencing my own difficult time whilst grieving the loss of my dear friend. Like so many of my patients, Kim was taken at the beginning of her life in a tragic road accident.

I wanted to be at work every day because I needed to be occupied and not alone. I was so lucky to have had a great support network on the ward. The families were so gracious with their compassion. They never hesitated to open their arms, ready to share in someone else's pain because in that moment of giving comfort, it temporarily took away their own pain.

It was about six weeks after Kim's death and I was struggling emotionally. I spoke little of my internal pain because I was surrounded by people much worse off than myself but trying to hold my pain inside was taking its toll.

I came to work and was allocated the same patient for the third day in a row. He had a debilitating terminal disease and was difficult to look after because of all the emotional turmoil he was experiencing. I understood his difficulty as being part of the process and as a professional; I dealt with the patient with the compassion and understanding that he deserved.

However, after the third day, I was emotionally drained and became unable to neither cope with his outbursts nor support him through them.

I could not console him at a time that I was carrying my own feelings of grief, and I felt incapable of caring for him. I had done exceptionally well up until then but I knew when I needed to step aside. At the same time, I felt the guilt of not being able to put my own feelings to the side because he was in fact dying and I was still standing and healthy. His diagnosis made me feel that my own pain was insignificant and feeling that, contributed to the reason that I attempted to continue caring for him. I also felt angry that not once did he stop to consider what might be going on in my life but that was unfair because he was the patient. I was the professional and what was happening to me was not supposed to get in the way. I felt the guilt of my thoughts as a professional and this added to my distress.

I had become a hard task master from early days particularly, on myself. I am a strong person and I expect a lot of myself but sometimes, the expectations were unrealistic. When I look back, I can see how the messages and my perception of things I learnt as a child were also impacting on my professional life. I think, too, that my personality contributed.

I learnt a lot on this ward about caring for our emotional well-being but applying those lessons to myself was not as easy as I thought. I was exceptional at caring for everyone else but pretty hopeless when it came to me. I believe the nursing profession views counselling as an adjunct to the healing of a visible wound but I failed to see the connection to myself because I did not have a wound that anyone could see.

'Why is it that we traditionally give so much attention to a visible weeping wound, yet give little consideration to an emotional wound on its own?'

I believe the biggest difference is that we can see the weeping wound. We can see it begin as a red and inflamed area that may be no bigger than a twenty cent piece. When we can see a wound, we have tangible evidence to support our pain or illness. We can therefore give the wound care and attention with or without medication. Then on a daily basis, we watch the skin heal over with little less than a blemish remaining. Our friends and families rally around to support us to get better and once the healing is done; they pull back their attention knowing that the healing process is complete.

An emotional wound is so different. Only you yourself know the extent or severity of the wound and regardless of how painful it is a high percentage of sufferers would not be as quick to seek help. I did not seek help for my grief, yet I was surrounded by the healing profession. No one could see my pain, so to everyone around me I looked OK. Every now and then, I may have a few tears and my colleagues would stop momentarily to share some compassion. After that, we were back caring for our patients again as if my moment of tears did not really occur.

I believe the human body is the most sophisticated piece of equipment that we are ever going to have total control over. We need to treat our bodies with the utmost respect and not ignore the signs and symptoms it shows us. These are the messages that something is wrong.

Whilst I tried to ignore my emotional wounds, it did not take long before my body responded to my lack of acknowledgement that I required some emotional healing. My body responded by sending me a strong physical message that I could not ignore. I was overcome with aching joints and an inability to put one foot in front of the other in a normal fashion. I was in intense pain and physically and emotionally exhausted. A colleague saw my pain and took me aside.

I quickly turned into a blubbering mess and broke my silence. I let out the bottled up feelings of grief and loss that I had for Kim.

Releasing my pain was a turning point for me. I felt relief that I had shared my thoughts and feeling of despair with someone else and I was in good hands.

I had tried to be that superhuman I had trained myself, so well to be. I comforted my patients and families by telling them to care for themselves emotionally and yet, I did not take my own advice. I was broken and had left it too long. I took holiday leave of six weeks to regain my physical and emotional strength. I was burnt out and in desperate need of repair.

I learnt the importance first hand of looking after my emotional wounds because if you don't, your body will stop you in the most debilitating way. I also believe that some illnesses or diseases can be worsened or accelerated by ongoing untreated stress on the body.

During my six-week period of recovery, I moved out of the hospital accommodation and in with a long time friend in a Sydney suburb of Carramar.

CHAPTER 12

RELATIONSHIPS—THE PICKET FENCE

> Celebrate every relationship you've ever had. For better or worse, your relationships are your best teachers.
>
> (Christiane Northrup)

I met my long time friend Sue when I was about twelve years old. She has had a big influence on me throughout my life. I have always admired and respected her ideals and beliefs. She is well grounded and doesn't need anyone else to make herself feel good. I was completely the opposite.

I was driven by gaining acceptance from those people around me. Sue was one of those people who accepted me in any shape or form because we had a solid friendship. She taught me a lot about relationships through our friendship, especially the importance of trust, acceptance, stability, respect, and unconditional love. I admired her ability to go out and get what she wanted. The time living with her put some emotional stability into my personal life, and now it was time to reassess my professional life. I decided a change in my work environment would be of benefit to me as I had spent a few years on the same ward.

As the saying goes 'A change is better than a holiday'.

I went to the newly opened burns unit of a major hospital. However, my time there was short-lived because I recognised that I was not emotionally equipped to deal with patients who were in constant pain. Their pain and suffering distressed me and sometimes I could not fix it for them. I liked to fix everyone. Their daily bath and extensive dressings could take up to seven hours some days and their suffering during that time was too much for me.

I am a professional and I recognised that I had chosen the wrong area of nursing. I have the utmost admiration for the nurses who work in that environment but it was not for me.

At the time I had another friend who was working in an extremely busy emergency department. I met Renata on a ward whilst she was a student nurse. We hit it off straight away, and I admired her because she was always willing to throw herself into new challenges and experiences. She often talked of her stable family environment, and I could see how this had influenced her relationships and friendships. We became close friends, and she soon talked me into working in emergency.

I was in fear of going to such a highly technical busy environment when I had no experience, but she had faith in my ability, so I thought 'what the heck' and took the plunge. I transferred to emergency and that is where I found my calling. I loved the excitement and adrenaline rush of not knowing what was going to come through the entrance doors. I loved working within a team with the aim to save a person's life and meticulously planning and prioritising each step to maximise, not only the patient's chance of survival but also the quality of their life if they did survive. This was the most satisfying time of my life. I felt respected and valued as a professional, and that crossed over into my personal life.

It was within a few short months that I met a man who treated me so different to all the others. I was attracted to his professionalism, kindness, and compassion. He was considerate and we had so much in common. I fell in love almost instantaneously, and within a short time, we had decided we wanted to spend the rest of our lives together. I felt he treated me like a princess, and I believed I had finally found what I was looking for in life.

Our relationship began how I imagined it as a child whilst sitting on my backyard swing when I would dream of falling in love and living happily ever after. I imagined a house full of love, laughter, and children. That was what all the fairytales portrayed would happen. The damsel in distress is rescued by the prince and then lives happily ever after. The fairytale ends at that point, sometimes depicting the scene of a wedding and other times it might just be the kiss that seals the romance. I grew up with this romantic vision of how life was meant to be. This vision was in stark contrast to what I saw as a child but within my heart I never gave up on that dream.

Even though I had found love, I still yearned for the acceptance and approval of my mother. She was the most significant person in my life, but it seemed the more independent I became, the less I felt her approval. I believe a daughter should have her mother in her life. That is what all the therapists say, all the studies say, and all the courts say. Mother, Mother, Mother.

As the years have passed from my childhood to adulthood and my achievements in life grew, I could still sense my mother's distance and I perceived this as non-acceptance of me. This yearning for approval left me wondering all these years what I had done wrong.

What was it that made me so undeserving of any recognition or acceptance?

I could not figure it out. My continued confusion around my mother left me holding on to the idea that I needed to achieve even more, to the point of exhaustion. I could not understand what it was I needed to do in order for her to accept me so I just kept trying harder but nothing I did seemed to make any difference.

The moments of humiliation for me continued well into adulthood when I became engaged to be married and I moved back home for a short period with the idea of saving money. I lived at home for only a few weeks until I realised it was not working out for me. I decided to move out again, but I delayed telling my mother until the day before the move to avoid a confrontation. This was a bad idea because the day I came to collect my belongings; I saw all my furniture sitting on the front footpath waiting for me. My father appeared and informed us that he could not help us load the truck because he would be in the dog house! He relented and helped us anyway. I collected every belonging that I had at their house and moved back with my friend Sue.

On my wedding day, the fairytale that I created in my mind as a small child had come true for me. As I stood at the altar in my beautiful white wedding gown and looked into his eyes,

I said the words 'till death do us part'.

I had complete faith in those words and believed them to be true and for a lifetime, I was committed to the complete package. Together to the end until one of us dropped off the perch or fell out of our rocking chairs.

Not long after I was married, my mother and father separated. My father had moved out of the family home and was sleeping in his car. I did not want to get involved in my parent's separation, but I could not have my father living as a homeless person. I allowed him to move in as a temporary arrangement until he found somewhere else more suitable.

It was not long before I realised I had put myself in the difficult position between my mother and father because I gave him a place to sleep. Each day, I listened to my father crying over the fact that he missed my mother and then on the other hand, my mother would phone and want to talk about the weather! This put me in an uncomfortable position and I felt further disapproval from my mother for allowing my father to stay with us. I also felt a sense of guilt from my father for the contact I had from my mother. It was a no win situation for me. I felt like I was expected by both my mother and father to choose one parent over the other. This was not something that I could do because I loved them both, and I did not feel it was my place to get involved because after all, they were meant to be the adults.

My relationship with my mother just kept spiralling and I seemed to make it my fulltime job to salvage it. My parents got back together after a short time apart and their relationship appeared to return to some normality.

It was a few years later that our daughter was born. My mother continued to remain emotionally distant. I believed it was because of something that I had done although she would never deny nor confirm that for me.

This left me guessing and in an untenable position because I was going to shelter the blame because that is what I had become accustomed too. The distant behaviour of my mother, the mixed messages, and her apparent disapproval added negativity to my world. I now had a beautiful daughter and for me, there was certainly nothing to be negative about. My daughter was so precious and my own special little pearl.

I wanted my mother in my life. I wanted my mother to share the beauty of my daughter, so I sort some counselling on my behalf and asked my mother to participate. She was willing to come to a session. Throughout the session, I listened to my mother talking about the pain in her life and the impact her relationships had had on her. She lived with an immense amount of guilt and grief from her own childhood. My mother had spoken to us previously when we were teenagers about her past but I had no understanding of her feelings or her pain. It was a harsh world she lived in at the time of her childhood but that was so many years later and here she was with a beautiful new grandchild. I did not understand why she could not move on from her past and take pleasure from her extended family. I listened intently to my mother's account of her pain, but I could not reach out to my mother. Her own pain was too intense and it was obvious to me that she was not going to be able to understand my pain when hers was all she could talk about. Only my mother could deal with her pain and at that point, I realised I just had to take a step back and live my life the best way I knew how, for the sake of my own family. My family had to be given priority.

I loved my mother, but I felt I had no choice but to love her from a distance. I knew I had to put that distance between us as I attempted to make my own life and bring up my own family. When our daughter was nearly seventeen months old, a job prospect came up interstate and I was quick to jump at the opportunity to move as far away as possible.

We moved to Tasmania for a work opportunity and it was like a breath of fresh air for me. I could finally have some breathing space from my many unsuccessful attempts to gain the approval and acceptance that I so desperately wanted. During this time, I heard very little from any of my family and it proved better that way for me. I received some regular letters from my father at one point, but I had not spoken to him for some time.

CHAPTER 13

MY FATHER'S LAST DAYS—A CRUEL TWIST

> I loved you dad and always did. I miss you dad and always will. The nurses let me see you, on your sick bed. You squeezed my hand and nodded your head. It was your sign to me that love shines through, unconditionally always, forever true. That day, I felt so much at peace, as some pain and hurt I did release. In my thoughts you will always be grand, in my memory I still hold your hand. I love you, dad.
>
> Sharon Gardiner

It was one day in 1993 when I heard news that my father was dying from a complication post surgery. I was not given the privilege to receive this information first hand and I am not really sure why, but nothing surprised me at the time.

I heard from my oldest brother that my father was a patient in the intensive care unit of a western Sydney hospital. I was told that his life support was going to be turned off and he was likely to die soon after that. My nursing experience told me that I should wait and see what the real situation was with my father but I was living in Tasmania so I had to consider the travelling time in my decision-making.

This was my father who I loved dearly. It did not matter to me what had happened in our lives between family members or circumstances. I was not going to just standby while my father died. I had to at least, have the chance to tell him that I loved him. I needed to do that for me and for him as well. The bond we shared could not be taken away by anybody.

I had little notice of his pending death and I soon realised the difficulty of that stretch of water between mainland Australia and Tasmania. I turned up at the airport in the morning in an attempt to catch an early flight, but to my dismay, I was told there were no seats available. I was not going to take that as an option, so I began desperate tearful negotiations with the airline staff. I did manage to get on one of the next flights, and I was so relieved, I gave them a thank you hug.

I remember clearly the stress and anxiety of being put in the untenable position, where I was excluded from any input into my father's last days. I was bewildered about the situation, but my mind was not focused on anything else other than going to see him. I felt that it was my right as a daughter and I was determined to see my father before he died. At this time, I could only think of my father, I had to see him, and I made that my mission.

On arrival in Sydney, I was met by a close friend Cathy who had been at my side when Kim died and many other times over the years. We were on our way to the hospital when I could feel the anxiety building. I felt shaky and nauseated, my palms were sweaty, and I was close to tears. I needed to see my father but on the other hand, I felt sick at the thought that I could end up in a confrontation with my mother. Cathy observed my anxious state and said,

'What are you more concerned about, seeing your father or your mother?'. I replied, 'My mother'.

It was a crazy family rift that had somehow evolved over years and years, but to be honest, I did not really even understand what it was all about.

That is one of the sad facts about family dynamics where the deterioration happens over an extended period. By that stage, the rift often becomes irreparable. I felt so strongly that I had to see my father in his dying days.

I can't imagine any punishment more severe than an attempt to deny a daughter of news regarding the life and death of her father. I felt I was being punished.

Just before visiting my father, I went to Cathy's house, which was very close to the hospital. I thought then that my anxiety level could not go any higher until I rang the intensive care unit. I wanted to know what time I could visit. I spoke with a member of the nursing staff and I was told in a few short words that they had never heard of their patient having another daughter. I was taken aback by the next question,

'Are you his step daughter?'

I found myself in a situation that I had to convince a stranger that I was in fact his blood daughter. This made me feel so humiliated and traumatised that I had been left out of what a tragic situation was involving my father.

I could see from my nursing experience that *my* feelings were not what the nurse was going to base her decision on in relation to allowing me to see my father. Her decision would be likely to be based on the welfare of the patient in her direct care. The difficultly that I could see from my nursing experience was that my father was unconscious, and therefore the next point of call would be to seek permission from his immediate family. At that moment, I realised that the ability for me to see my father was going to be dependent on a mother that had excluded me in the first instance. I did not care about my mother's reasoning at that time.

I was beside myself with the fear that I would not get the opportunity to say goodbye to my father. I was becoming desperate, but it just did not get any better. I was then informed by that same intensive care nurse that I should seek help from the social work department as I was not the patient's immediate family. I was flabbergasted to say the least completely distraught and starting to feel defeated. I hung up the phone and was ready to give up, believing in some way that I did not deserve to see my father. I was so upset because I had this overwhelming need to see my father before he died. I became confused and had difficulty understanding what was going on.

Thank goodness, my friend Cathy was not going to take no for an answer. She dialled the phone number again and told me to ask to speak to the nurse who was looking after my father. I was able to speak to my father's nurse and he said in his kind compassionate voice, 'Come and see your father in the rest time, no one else is allowed. I will let you in'.

My heart sunk and tears welled up in my eyes. We rushed straight to the hospital. I walked through the hospital corridors with apprehension because I wanted to avoid any confrontation with my mother. It was not the appropriate time or place. The situation was emotional for all involved, but at that time, my focus was on seeing my father. The first thing I did was speak to the nurse and then I walked over to my father's bed and looked at him.

He was a sorry sight and looked very ill. I saw the many tubes coming out of his mouth, nose, and chest. I looked at the machine that controlled his breathing. It operated in a rhythmic manner, making noises that coincided with the rise and fall of his chest. I had seen this many times during my nursing experience, but the circumstances were now so personal to me because the patient was my beloved father.

Whilst I attempted to hold back tears from running down my face, I spoke to him in a gentle quivering voice. I was surprised to see my father open his eyes and look at me. I could see and feel that he was aware of my presence. He could not speak with his voice, but his eyes said all that needed to be said. I could see the love in his eyes and I believe he could see the love in mine. The moment when our eyes connected was an important moment for both of us, and I believe it brought us both some closure. I loved my father so much and had missed him being in my life.

I took his hand and held it in mine. I promised him that when he got better that we would work out all this stupid family stuff and that we would be together again. I said that to him knowing that he was going to die and there was little chance that any of the family stuff would be sorted. I wanted him to have some hope and comfort. I wanted to give myself some hope and comfort.

I sat with my father and held his hand, whilst my eyes frequently tracked back to the hands of the clock that sat above the entry doors. I was aware that every movement of the minute hand counted down, how many minutes I had left in my father's life. I knew I was getting minutes closer to the last time I would hold my father's hand, the last time I could see his eyes look into mine, and the last time he would hear my voice.

Although my father's eye contact was intermittent, I felt the emotional intensity of the moment for both of us. He was tired, partially sedated, and needed his rest. I sat next to his bed waiting for his waking moments. I stroked his warm freckly arm and listened to the rhythm of his breathing.

The clock ticked down and it was time for me to leave because the rest period was over. I told my father, I loved him very much and I was sorry for all the unresolved issues that had gone on in our family. I told him that my brother also sent his love. I kissed him on the cheek, and I felt a lump in my throat start to make my swallowing difficult. I contemplated the thought that I would not see him again. Walking away from his bedside was the hardest few steps I had to take.

There were only thoughts of the father that I loved that day, and I am so thankful to that nurse who gave me the opportunity to spend time with my dying father. I won't forget the compassion and non-judgement he showed me. I felt the nurse cared for me that day and my friend was my strength. I am very grateful to them both. My friend Cathy gave me the support I needed to be courageous and seek out what was important to me. She stood by me until I got what I came for.

I returned to Tasmania to my own family, and three days later, I received a message on my answering machine that my father had died. I felt very sad, but at the same time, a sense of peace came over me that I was able to spend those precious moments with him.

This was a major turning point for me. I had my own children at the time and I could not understand how any parent could attempt to deny a child their right to see their father, whatever the circumstances. It was beyond my comprehension. I was proud of myself and my friend that day for standing up and persisting with my need to see my father in his dying days.

I realised then that I could only love my mother from a distance and therefore, since my father's death nineteen years ago, I have spoken to her only a handful of times.

I believe my mother's decision to keep my father's illness from me was a cruel mistake. I know that she had her own reasons and I respect that but I believe she was wrong. I realised that I had achieved my purpose of seeing my father and that was all that mattered at the time, but I felt so hurt.

The decision my mother made to deny me the right to see my father would play a pivotal role in my own decisions some years later.

CHAPTER 14

THE FAIRY TALE—TILL DEATH DO US PART

> If you can learn from every relationship and understand how it came into your life, then no relationship needs to be remembered with regret.
>
> (Deepak Chopra)

My husband was a wonderful man who was a good provider, a good father, and a good friend. He was very supportive of me and whatever I wanted to achieve in life.

He loved our children dearly and enjoyed spending time with them. We had so much in common and that maintained a good friendship between us. I supported him in his study and work as he supported me in my endeavours. We both encouraged our children to be the best that they could and we gave them all the love we had in our hearts.

I had come from a childhood that taught me many lessons about bringing up children, in particular how *not* to bring up a child. I was determined to bring my children up with unconditional love, respect, and acceptance. I wanted to give them a secure home environment where they never had to experience instability.

My husband brought his own lessons from his childhood and together we did the best that we could to give our children a happy caring childhood.

We had no instructions just like many parents, but we believed the best gift that we could give our children was a childhood minus all the not so memorable moments of our own childhood. I was determined not to repeat the same mistakes of my own parents.

It was when my children were around six and four years of age that I knew that something was missing from my marriage and this made me sad. I had all the things in life that I ever wanted and this should have been enough for me, but deep down, I felt a feeling of emptiness. What I was looking for in my fairytale was just not there. I had a wonderful friendship with my husband but that was all I felt it was. The intimacy that I desired and wanted from a relationship was missing.

> Intimacy means that we're safe enough to reveal the truth about ourselves in all its creative chaos. If a space is created in which two people are totally free to reveal their walls, then those walls, in time, will come down.
>
> (Marianne Williamson)

I tried many times to describe my emotions, but I struggled to get my message across. This frustrated me even further because I felt like I did not have a voice and therefore what I was trying to say appeared unimportant. I felt powerless to change anything and therefore undeserving of the effort to even try.

At the time I was feeling this way, I took a trip to Sydney where I spent some time with friends. During that trip, I spent time on my own reflecting on my life. I was unhappy deep down inside where no one could see. I didn't feel that I could return to my marriage. I felt there was little hope of saving my relationship and I believed that I did not have a voice that would be listened to. When I tried to speak out, it seemed to me that my words were left unheard. I had little understanding of my own emotions, so how was I going to explain that to another person? I found it difficult to express my feelings openly because I needed to avoid confrontation or conflict at all costs even though there was no threat of it.

I did some thinking in those four days away, and I thought long and hard about my own childhood and the instability that I endured. I had to think about my children and the good life that they had. I was not miserable by any means and considered my life to be pretty stable. I had that family unit that I always wanted and I cherished that. I had a good kind man who loved us all. I wanted my children to have that love that we could give them as a family and that was the driving force for my return. My friends supported me at that time, whatever my decision but I believe I did the right thing by returning home to my marriage. I cannot deny that the next ten years of my life remained happy, but in my heart I always felt that there was still something missing.

I listened to the stories of my friend's and their struggles in their relationships, but they spoke differently of their concerns. They spoke of husbands who wanted intimacy and affection and their constant battle to distract them. I was left thinking that there was something wrong with me that I was not desired in the same manner and to me that just compounded my feeling of being undeserving.

I had gone from craving love, affection, and approval in my formative years to feeling rejected as a wife over many years. I felt so undesirable and undeserving and therefore this added to my unhappiness as well as making me reluctant to talk about my feelings. I was bewildered.

Had I just been too tied up with the image of a fairytale? Was I so wrapped up in that image that I had lost a grip on real life? Was a relationship between two people in equal shares? My fairytale was disintegrating gradually over a period of time until I no longer felt part of it. My children became the main focus because they loved me unconditionally and in their eyes, I was beautiful. My children brought me great joy always. When I played with them, I could be just like a child too and we laughed and giggled and did silly things. I worked hard to please everyone in a hope that things in my life would get better.

Does that sound familiar to you? Was I just repeating the same scenario as I did when I was trying to please my mother? If I did everything to make everyone else happy then I felt I would be accepted and receive what it was that I felt was missing?

Life played out on a daily basis as did every other household with the routine of children to school, parents to work, and the dog lying around all day. Then home from school, work, dinner, chores, and more of the dog lying around. Bedtime came quick enough and the next day brought much the same. This went on like a broken record being played over and over again, day in and day out. Very little was changing.

It was a Saturday morning that I picked up the Australian newspaper and saw an advertisement for mature-aged applicants to join the NSW Police.

I said to my husband, 'The NSW Police are advertising for mature age people.'

He said, 'Why don't you apply?'

I said, 'How would that work out with full time shift work and the children?'

He said, 'They are old enough now.'

I said, 'Do you think it would work?'

He said, 'Yes, you have been talking about joining the police for the past seventeen years. Why don't you apply?'

I said, 'Have I really?'

He said, 'Yes, for as long as I can remember'

It was from then on that I started my journey towards joining the police service.

I had a renewed passion in my life, and even though I had a life that I felt essentially happy with, I still had an empty feeling inside of me. I likened my marriage to be more of a good friendship, and even though I tried to speak about that often, I felt my words remained unheard. I felt so lonely within my relationship. We became strangers. My emotions were so mixed around that time in my life it was like I had given up on my own true happiness. My efforts to change things appeared fruitless. I wondered if what it was I wanted in my life was unrealistic and unreachable. I believed that I should be grateful for the life I was living, but at the same time, I was feeling incredibly lonely and unhappy. It was for me, a confusing time and I did not have the answers.

CHAPTER 15

THE PENNY DROPPED—
THIS STARTED THE WHEELS OF CHANGE

> We gain strength and courage and confidence by each experience in which we really stop to look fear in the face . . . we must do that which we think we cannot.
>
> (Eleanor Roosevelt)

I had a fascination for anything to do with police from an early age. My first memory of anything police was the police horses at public events that I went to with my family. The horses would always be out amongst the crowds. Their huge, meticulously groomed bodies towered over the crowds. The police officers sat well planted on their polished saddles looking rather distinguished in their immaculate uniforms. To a young child, it looked like the best and most important job in the world. My mother liked them because they reminded her of the horse guards at Buckingham Palace.

I can recall the many police officers whose figures appeared at our front door on numerous occasions whilst I was growing up. There were the ones who came knocking to collect unpaid fines or those that came in response to my parent's arguments. I remember so distinctly the police officer that visited our house on the day I was cowering in the corner so frozen with fear.

It was our local police officers that investigated the disappearance of my neighbour who we called Aunty. She had befriended a man whilst he was in prison. When he was released on weekend leave, he murdered her and dumped her body in bushland. Whilst she remained missing, I remember seeing the police officers at her house twenty-four hours per day for days on end. When they walked around her back garden, they often stopped to chat with me over our fence. I was quick to volunteer to feed her cat, just so I could chat to them when they sat in their shiny police car parked across her driveway. The police officers were always very tall, broad shouldered, and dressed immaculately. Their hair was always cut short and they were clean shaven. I was star struck by them.

I went to her funeral at the church next door to St Marys police station and saw the investigating police and the same police officers attending the sombre occasion. I thought that was such an important gesture for her family who were trying to deal with her tragic death.

The special memories I have of the police have stayed with me all my life. I was an impressionable young teenager at the time so it is no wonder that I dated several police officers whilst working at the Opera House and during my nurses training. The night before my final nursing exam, I was out with a police officer till 4 a.m. I went home, caught two hours sleep, studied till it was time to leave, and then sat my exam. I failed unfortunately, but I was not going to tell anyone why. It was a hard lesson to learn so the next time I studied hard and sat the exam again three months later and I passed.

In 1983 after the completion of my nurses training I went on an overseas trip, and when I returned to Australia I could not get a job as a nurse. This gave me the opportunity to enquire about joining the police service.

At that time, I went to the local police station and spoke with the desk sergeant. He gave me a few tips about the fitness level required. I went straight down to the local park and attempted a sprint to see what I might get. I was quick to realise that fitness was not my forte and therefore I should put that idea to the back burner and persist with finding a nursing job.

I did eventually get a nursing job in the Blue Mountains. As I got back into my nursing career, I came into contact with police officers on a daily basis and therefore over the years I started to go out with a few. I was always inspired by their stories whilst in uniform and their ability to have some fun outside of work. They were one of the most respected groups of individuals when I was in my early teens and twenties. I loved everything to do with the police so when my husband informed me that I had been talking about joining for seventeen years, I guess I could confidently say that it was a dream of mine since childhood.

I started the academic study through Charles Sturt University as a distance education student. That meant I could complete my studies whilst remaining at home and in my current employment.

I was very fortunate to have such a supportive family at the time with my two children and husband. I will always be appreciative of their support, particularly his.

I was confident that I could meet the academic requirements of the course but not so confident with the fitness requirements. I was determined though and therefore started on a fitness regime that would leave most people for dead. I had to learn to love pain and running. I hated running. I struggled with every exercise and for a while it seemed that I had no hope, but I was determined to reach every goal and every level that was required of me. I was forty-two years of age and this was going to be the challenge of my life, and I was excited. I had everyone in my life barracking for me.

I knew I could not do the fitness on my own, so I went to my local gym to get some professional help. I informed them of my goal and that started the ball rolling. I ended up with a team of people ready to support me and help me to achieve my dream. They designed our plan of attack, which unfortunately included running.

I was riddled with self-doubt that I could obtain the required standard of fitness because I had never been that fit before. It was so important for me that I had people around me that believed in my ability. At the time I did not believe I could achieve my goals because I always looked too far ahead. Instead, I needed to just concentrate on knocking each goal off as I achieved them. One of my trainers gave me this quote; however, it was not till much later after I had achieved so much that I really understood the full meaning.

> Most people never run far enough on their first wind to find out they have a second. Give your dreams all you've got and you'll be amazed at the energy that comes out of you.
>
> (William James)

My team of supporters from my gym stood by me from the beginning of my journey. When I started I could not do one push up, one full sit up, my flexibility was under the expected requirement, my cardio fitness rather nonexistent and I had never run in my life. It took about ten months of complete dedication and persistence to get there. My trusty trainers were with me until I reached my goal and achieved my dream. All that self-doubt was just such a waste of energy, but I could not overcome it even when I saw my results on paper and in the mirror.

My own self-doubt and fear was part of an array of messages tucked away in my subconscious just waiting to sabotage my efforts. I avoided physical activity at school because there was always someone better. The teachers only picked the best students for their teams because it was all about winning. I hated swimming carnivals because we were forced to participate.

After achieving the minimum fitness requirement, I was accepted into the second session of police training in September 2003. This meant leaving my normal life as a wife and mother to attend the Goulburn police college for three months of intensive training, Monday to Friday. The hours varied but in most cases, the days were long and arduous. The college is set up well and had good facilities to get the training done.

I was apprehensive about what challenges might be ahead of me, but at the same time, I was extremely excited about the unknown. The training consisted of a combination of physical fitness, officer safety, and operational policing both practical and observation. The second session also saw the academic requirements become more job focused rather than just theory. I had no idea whether I would make the grade, but I knew that I had come this far and I was going to try my best and put in the hard yards to get through.

On the Sunday prior to my first day at the college, our families were allowed on site to see where we would be spending the next twelve weeks. I liked that because I thought it was important for my children to have some insight into the challenges ahead of me. They too were making sacrifices in their own lives, so I was able to pursue my dream.

The residences were basic but adequate. I was in one of the front towers on the middle floor with sixteen rooms and three showers and toilets. The room was very basic with a bed, desk, chair, and wardrobe. Each room had a window and heating was paramount. The weather in Goulburn was well known for its harsh extremes in heat and cold, but winter was particularly unkind. There was a communal lounge room and small kitchen area, industrial-type laundry facilities, and a well-equipped gym within the college. All meals were provided by the large cafeteria. Our families were allowed to tour unrestricted areas so they could understand some of the challenges ahead.

On the Monday of the first week, we were allocated our classes and met our main tutor. I was placed into a class with eighteen other student police officers of varying age. I was one of the oldest in the class beside another female but not long into the course she left the college and her policing career, leaving me as the oldest student in the class at a ripe age of forty-three.

My classmates appeared well rounded from varying backgrounds. This aspect added to my excitement because I had always been fascinated hearing what other people had done or achieved in their lives. I love meeting new people and because we were all in the same boat, we started with a level playing field. This meant we could help each other from the same beginning point.

The first day went very quickly and it was not long before, we realised that the true test of our capabilities was about to begin. The timetable was so full that you just got dragged along like a whirlwind, but we were together in the whirlwind as a class. My classmates were wonderful and caring. There was the diversity of skills and life experience that added to the special bonds that we would ultimately form, the longer we spent together.

I had confidence in myself that I could achieve good results in the academic component of the course, but the physical and tactical side was different altogether. I was not so confident with my capabilities and in fact absolutely scared beyond words. Regardless of my fear, I was completely committed to giving the training my best effort even if it killed me.

The weeks were transformed from exciting and thrill-seeking to long and arduous. The timetable was gruelling, and there was no room for falling behind. One lesson would be based in the classroom fairly easy paced and the next could be in the padded rooms practicing anything from handcuffing to knife defence tactics.

Amidst all the challenges came the reality that our families were at home without us. I thought of my children many times during the day but especially the last thing at night before I shut my eyes and as soon as I woke in the morning. I pictured them having breakfast and heading off to school.

One morning I woke at the usual time of 5 a.m. I stood to look at the photos of my children I had spread over the wall when I was disturbed by loud deep voices in a rhythmic tone getting closer and closer. I went to my window and was taken aback by the dawning of a beautiful day over the grass paddocks that surrounded the residences. At that same time, I saw a group of men marching past, chanting and stepping in rhythm, looking seriously fit and masculine.

I had not seen a sight like this in real life and I couldn't believe my luck (after all it was 5 a.m. in the morning). The sight sent a shiver down my spine wiping away any thoughts of my children and highlighting to me the many bonuses I could possibly experience while I was at the college. I knew my children would be OK, so I decided to concentrate on the important things in life like the eye candy I had just been blessed to see. I knew there was a reason I got up that time of the morning to go for a run. When you don't particularly like running especially at 5.30 a.m., any motivation is welcomed.

My fitness was letting me down somewhat and although I gave it all, I found it difficult to juggle everything and still be standing at the end of the day, but I knew I had to dig deep inside me whatever it took. I think the universe sent me the eye candy just to give me some relief and make me realise that I needed to appreciate the fact that I was living my dream.

That sight, first thing in the morning certainly put a bounce in my step for the rest of the day and gave me a bit of a lift for that early morning run.

I felt like I started my time at the police college on the back foot because I had little belief in myself and such a terrible fear of failure. On the other hand, I felt that I could tackle anything that was asked of me and I would give it all I had. It was not long before I realised that my classmates had fears of their own and that reassured me because a lot of them were half my age!

People around me seemed to believe in me far more than I think I believed in myself. I had layers of self-doubt lingering constantly always ready to smash my confidence and my dream of becoming a police officer. In my mind, this was my only opportunity and I was determined not to fail because chances like this only happen once in a lifetime. Every day of intense training, I started to conquer so many things that I never thought I would ever do in my wildest dreams. My accomplishments and achievements just kept adding up one by one.

There was a day I remember when, our class was learning tactical moves in the padded rooms. During this session, the instructor wanted to make sure that we all knew how to fall 'softly'. I had never thought fall and softly went together and I felt nervous but the worst was yet to come. The next thing I heard was forward rolls.

It was the mention of the phrase 'forward rolls' that caused a chemical reaction in me similar to when I was confronted by my first serious trauma patient. I had a burst of adrenaline to help me to cope with my fear, but at the same time I could not show it. A trauma patient does not want to see fear in the nurse's face nor do your classmates want to know that you are terrified. My emotional reaction came when I remembered the wise words of my mother when she told me as a young child, 'never do forward rolls because if you did them wrong, you could break your neck'

I was standing there with no time to think about my fear and no way of getting out of it. I quickly found myself on the padded mat doing a forward roll in a fairly clumsy manner. After some instruction and tips, I continued doing those forward rolls to perfection until I had completed about fifty. I can't describe the achievement that I felt after that session. I had overcome a long time fear regarding a simple roll on the mat to just doing it and all it took was a two-hour session. I was stoked and quietly ecstatic!

I find it intriguing that I could have had such a fear for most of my life and it really was quite unfounded. I am sure my mother had my best interests at heart when I was a child, but I believe this is a good example of how perceptions and beliefs of others can influence us. Having the fear that I was going to break my neck really did dampen the enjoyment of my accomplishment. I think that most things in life that are important to us can create some degree of fear. It is whether the fear is proportionate to what it is you want to achieve or conquer.

I feared breaking my neck more than anything, but I also feared not succeeding in what I was asked to do. The latter was a worse thought for me. I had to trust that the instructor knew his job and then I had to just get on with it. That day was significant for me because I had put aside a long time unfounded fear and made a conscious decision to make my own choice. That choice was to push through the fear because I just had to do it. If others could do forward rolls and not break their neck, then so could I.

During my time in Goulburn, I experienced many of these moments and it was a culmination of all those moments that I started to recognise a pattern of thinking within myself. I listened to the positive messages coming my way from both my peers and the staff, and I enjoyed their immense support. I was humbled at the admiration shown to me by my classmates and colleagues. I felt so supported and had formed a special bond with so many people. On the whole, I found the admiration shown to me by my classmates, intriguing.

CHAPTER 16

SELF DOUBT OVERTOOK ME—AGAIN

> When the going gets tough, those with a dream keep going
> (Ben Feldman)

One night around the eight week point, I started to feel overwhelmed with everything around me. The timetable was gruelling, assignments were due, and every day I was confronted by some new personal challenge. I was exhausted and began on a spiral of self-doubt and negative thinking.

I decided to take the easy way out and go home because it was all too much. I grabbed my handbag and keys, locked my room, and quietly opened the fire escape door. I started to walk down the stairs and I came face-to-face with one of the girls on my floor. She stopped and looked at my handbag.

She said, 'Where are you going?' I looked at her and said nothing. She said, 'You're going home, aren't you?'

I did not answer her directly, but instead, I told her I would be back in a few days. She stopped me in my tracks and tried to talk me out of it. We all knew that missing a few days of classes within such a tight schedule meant the end to your time at Goulburn. It was impossible to catch up classes.

The next thing I knew, I was surrounded by such a lovely group of girls that genuinely cared what happened to me. They told me how I inspired them and they shared stories of their own struggles with fear and self-doubt. They informed me that they were not going to let me go home even if one of them had to sleep in my room on the floor next to me. I was again humbled by their compassion and concern for me.

I realised in Goulburn that the training was about a group of people and not the individual, and when one person hurt, everyone rallied around them. This was the beginning of the police family that I came so familiar with after graduation.

I decided to stay that night because I had come so far and after a visit to my family over the weekend, I settled back into the routine. After a weekend at home, I returned to Goulburn with a book in hand called '*Feel the Fear and Do it anyway*' by Susan Jeffers. I was desperate.

One day whilst I was heading to the bathroom in the residence, I ran into one of my classmates. We were living on the same floor for weeks and we had no idea. Stacey was married at the time and her home was close by, so she spent most of her week travelling to and from. Stacey and I did not have much to do with each other within the class, for no particular reason we were just acquaintances, but when I met her this day that all changed.

We started talking and were drawn to each other instantly. We had a lot in common with the policing aspect of our lives, but we soon discovered that we had so much in common on a personal level. We became friends that night and this would be the turning point in the direction I was heading both professionally and personally. Stacey spoke of her admiration for me and my achievements and I was humbled again, but these comments still caused an uncomfortable reaction within me. I believed what she was saying was sincere, but I found it very confronting hearing positive comments about myself.

The support and admiration I received started to come on a daily basis from many different sources, and I started to feel bewildered and a little intrigued as to my uncomfortable reactions to them. I still could not quite pin point exactly what was happening to me and what the reactions meant, so I started to listen closer to the messages I was hearing in my head.

The self-doubt, the lack of faith in myself, the guilt of being away from my family, and a feeling that I did not deserve the praise I was getting were just some of the many thoughts I was having. At the same time, I was hearing my own familiar negative messages. I was being told conflicting things from a group of people who knew little about me. I was experiencing so many amazing moments. I was overcoming many obstacles and was determined that if I did not get them the first time, I would just dig deeper so I did not fail the next time. That is just what had to be done, so I just did it.

Every week I missed my family, and when I went home to see them, they were very supportive of me, but each time I went home, I would notice a change in my perception of things. My children were as wonderful as always, but it was my relationship with my husband, which was changing. I started to realise that I had made many achievements in my life but I felt these went unnoticed. My home environment did not give me the same level of positive reinforcement or satisfaction that I was receiving from complete strangers. I remained confused about my thoughts because I was unsure of what they meant. I put my thoughts aside to enable me to complete my training. In some way, I thought that once I returned home, I would be the same person that I was when I left three months earlier.

I had started to make good progress with the officer safety training and the next challenge was our firearm training. I had not seen a real gun prior to entering the college. The fact that I was going to have one issued to me under my name was daunting but at the same time, exciting. The pistol range was quite intimidating for me because of the safety requirements, the tight timetable, and the fact that there was no turning back. The range represented the reality of my dream. If I could master the use of a firearm and pass the requirements, then I knew I was going to make it.

My attitude at the beginning of the training was from a point of fear; however, with the help of the professionalism and expertise of the instructors, I was able to turn that fear around to a little glimmer of enjoyment. I did manage to pass my final shoot and obtain the required score on the target. I kept my target sheet as a memento of another achievement and today it hangs on the back of my door at home.

I was so proud of all my achievements, but I never took anything in Goulburn for granted. The whole journey was so challenging and it was not over until I had passed everything. As the twelve weeks started coming to an end and the exams were full steam ahead, I had to face my last chance at the fitness testing. I had failed to make the required amount of points in week eight so it was make or break time. I had passed everything so far but I felt exhausted and not looking forward to this last hurdle.

The beep test was in the morning before our law exam. The beep test is an endurance test over a twenty metre flat course. You start at the twenty metre marker and in line with the beep sound, you had to make it to the opposite twenty metre marker and place your foot on the marker before you heard the next beep sound. Each time you heard a triple beep, the levels changed and the speed increased. So when you completed level one, you would expect the speed to increase slightly for level two. The speed built up for each level. The pass mark was 5.2, but I needed much more than that to gain the overall point scores.

There was one thing about the training and that was the pressure that was loaded on us time and again. I think this was their way of testing us under duress and it worked. I was not only under duress but shattered mentally and physically.

Anyway regardless of that, I had to be down on the parade ground in the early hours of the morning to do the beep test. There was no point in complaining because that was wasted energy. I turned up to the parade ground and I saw a group of my classmates had come down to cheer me on and that made me feel so special. I really appreciated their support.

I did pass the required 5.2 in the beep test but I fell short of level 7.2, which placed pressure on me to make up the points from the other elements of the testing. This was going to prove difficult because I had several weaknesses to overcome but it was possible if I could pull that little bit extra out of me somewhere.

Unfortunately, I failed to get the required points. This meant that I could not graduate with my class and was very disappointing for me as well as my classmates. I felt pretty devastated myself, but I could see their deflated expressions when they realised that one of their own was not going to be on the parade ground with them. We were like a family and when one of the members hurt then everyone does. I was upset but realistically for me, I was physically spent. I could see the positives that I would at least get to spend Christmas with my family instead of starting the job, two days before Christmas. I was not the only one that failed and I had the option to return for the next session and be retested. I had to see the positives of what I had achieved and be pretty pleased with myself. The other people who failed were just as disappointed as me.

I could have gone home at that time, but I wanted to stay the rest of the week with my class mates and support them. I also wanted them to see that I was going to be OK. After a few drinks at the bar with my mates, I returned to my room a little deflated and quite intoxicated. Soon after, I got a knock on the door from Stacey. She had left her phone at the local pub and wanted me to drive her there to collect it. I laughed because there was no way I could drive. We decided to walk and took a shortcut through the horse paddock. The grass was long, it was dark and we could not see where we were walking but it did not bother us because we had conquered the unknown before. As we walked, we chatted about our achievements. We laughed about all the challenges that it took to get to where we were today, but sadly, we knew that the time was coming close where we had to say goodbye.

I had experienced the most incredible journey, but at the time I did not realise the enormity of it all. A failure was not what I planned for but I was not going to be beaten especially after pushing through so many fears.

It was time to say goodbye to all my friends and class mates. This was just a temporary goodbye because I knew that most of us would keep in touch. I slowly packed up my room and was met by Stacey before she headed off home. She had become my rock whilst at Goulburn and a true friend. She handed me a card with some gerbera flowers on the front. They were my favourite because of their vibrant colours.

I sat to read what she had written. This time the words were written and therefore I could not misinterpret their meaning or choose to disregard them.

As I read the words, my eyes welled up and tears of joy as well as sadness ran down my face.

To my dearest Shazza,

Well, unfortunately the day has come we all have to leave this place and go home. I will truly miss seeing you every day, our lunches, and special nights out, all now treasured memories of the great unique friendship we have shared. Sharon, you have shown commitment, perseverance, and strength of character that is rare and I have been in admiration of these qualities that you possess during our police academy journey together. Whilst it is extremely hard not to share this final step with you, I am positive there is no goal you cannot reach, and that this is merely an opportunity for you to have a relaxing break. Thank you for your friendship, I'm confident you are destined for many successful years in the police. Don't lose sight of the end of the tunnel, you have achieved countless heights, knock this last one over, and get out there, if anyone can do it Shaz, you can! Lots of hugs and kisses,

Stacey

I kept the card and will always treasure those words. I felt blessed by her kindness and appreciated her comments, but I felt she was writing about someone other than me. I just could not accept these good things as the truth.

As hard as it was for me, not to be with my classmates on graduation I was not going to miss their moment of glory. I felt so connected to them and I was proud of their achievements. As I drove into the college gates on the day of their graduation, the tears rolled down my face. The tears were for two reasons, one of them was for the sadness that I was not there beside my mates, and the other was the happiness I felt for all of them. They were an incredibly professional group of young men and women who I felt privileged to stand beside. It was just not meant to be for me on that graduation day but my turn would come.

I went home knowing that I had a few months grace before I would return to Goulburn. I really enjoyed the time with my family at Christmas, the sleeping in, the home-cooked meals, and the constant chatter of my children. I had though made a commitment to myself to complete my dream. It was in the January that I had to return to Goulburn to register my interest for a second attempt at the required fitness level.

It was on that day in Goulburn that I met up with several of my fellow students from my session. We claimed the tag of 'retreads' as many did before us and were a force to be reckoned with. We were aiming for the next graduation in late April.

I sat next to a pretty young lady who had failed her firearms. I remembered her briefly whilst at the college; however, our paths never crossed because we were in different classes. Her name was Kristy and we became and still are what she calls 'The bestest friends'. Kristy's positive attitude was the most striking thing about her. I was taken by her beautiful smile and caring attitude. She was bubbling with fun and that drew me to want to get to know her better.

We parted that day with each other's phone numbers, and I returned to my fitness training with the help of a local trainer. Kristy enrolled herself in one of the shooting clubs. We made a pact with each other that we would make a comeback. I ran with my trainer three times per week and the other days I went to the gym and ran some more. Kristy completed her training at the pistol club and we returned to Goulburn to conquer this last challenge. We both succeeded and graduated together in April 2004. I had not long celebrated my forty-fourth birthday.

When it came to graduation day, some of my classmates made the journey to Goulburn to see me graduate, and I felt so privileged to have them by my side this time. I enjoyed the day with my family and friends, but the enormity of it all was completely surreal. I had made it and I was officially a serving member of the NSW Police. I found this hard to believe.

I was still trying to piece together my conflicting emotions in relation to the positive messages that I was receiving so frequently. My time at Goulburn was life changing, and I learnt so many things about myself that I had never known previously. The first thing I learnt about myself was that I could achieve anything that I set my mind to. I persevered with my fitness and it paid off because I got there in the long run.

Amongst the celebrations of my achievement and the sincere compliments I was receiving from people, I was still a little bewildered. I felt in conflict with myself because, on a personal level, I could not relate to the type of compliments that I was hearing. I started to feel people's appreciation for the type of person I was, and that was something that I could not relate to either. I got the approval of everyone around me at Goulburn, but in my personal life, I was still searching for approval. I changed so much because of the experience. I wondered if I was able to return home the same person. I was intrigued that a whole group of people that I had not met before could be in awe of my achievements. Yet I felt insignificant and lonely in my personal life. I knew in myself that the person who everyone saw at Goulburn was the beginnings of the authentic me. The person I used to be before I placed so much emphasis on approval. In doing that I lost myself in the chase for it.

I was now a police officer and about to be initiated into a whole new world. I was going to be back working full-time in a new career, new environment, and surrounded by new and exciting daily tasks. I realised there was going to be little time for contemplation of my thoughts. I was living my dream, and that thought alone made it hard to keep my feet planted firmly on the ground.

CHAPTER 17

ON THE JOB—A SURREAL EXPERIENCE

> The highest point of achievement yesterday is the starting point of today
>
> (Motto of Paulist Fathers)

My first day as a police officer was exciting but at the same time surreal. It was a day of induction and orientation, a time to meet the boss and hear his expectations of us. On the first day, I was allocated a buddy to look after me essentially for the first six weeks while I found my feet and believe me, I did not let him out of my sight. I was excited but petrified at the same time.

In my first week, I was working with my buddy and another probationer when we were patrolling the Broadway end of George Street in the city's CBD. My buddy spotted a minor offence and wanted to pull over so we could have a chat to a male person. We wanted to stop our vehicle in the other direction. It was at that time I heard a siren. I was driving, so I was cautious that an emergency vehicle was approaching us. I was checking all the mirrors, waiting for a glimpse of the vehicle with the siren. I said to my buddy,

'Can you hear that siren because I cannot see which direction it's coming from?'

Laughter immediately broke out in the cabin of our vehicle when my colleagues realised what I had said. My buddy replied, 'That is our siren'.

I laughed and said, 'Really? I am having trouble just even thinking that I am driving a police vehicle and wearing this uniform, let alone thinking that we have a siren.'

We laughed and laughed for some time and I realised then that I needed some adjustment time to get used to the idea that I was living my dream and every now and then, I had to remind myself that I was a police officer. The feeling was so fantastic.

I loved the city environment and I felt proud to work with such a dedicated bunch of people who really cared about the community. There was not a day that went past that most of us felt that being in the job was a privilege. I was absorbed in my new career, and I was getting good feedback from my peers in relation to my work.

It was my personal life that was creating the biggest challenges for me so it was time to put the pieces of my life together. I had started to recognise some of my patterns of thinking and I spent some considerable time thinking about what it was in my relationship that just did not fit with me anymore.

About two months into my policing career, the penny dropped and I realised I had become a victim of my own past and I was reliving the patterns of the past in my present relationships.

I was looking to someone else to give me the approval that I had searched for my entire life. I became so buried in the notion that I would get what I felt I deserved that I lost sight of who I really was and by doing that, I essentially put my own happiness in the control of outside sources.

It was for me just a repetitious, habitual way of thinking that was slowly decaying who I was. I had attracted to me the type of relationships that supported my negative thought patterns. I was in a different world in the police service where I felt that my authentic self was shining through, but in my other life as a wife, I felt far from authentic. I was just surviving within a marriage that I felt gave me little purpose other than to care for two wonderful bright and happy children. I realised that I needed to reconnect with my authentic self. I was living a life different to what my soul was yearning for and therefore I made the decision to leave a life that I was so familiar with.

> Courage is the power to let go of something familiar
> (Raymond Lindquist)

I had been in the police service for around four months when my marriage ended. My police colleagues helped me through some of the hardest times in my life, and I felt that I was in the right place at the right time to face the future alone. I knew that I had achieved so much and I was confident I would get through the tough times ahead, but I had no idea what was about to hit me. As time went by and I gained greater insight into myself, I realised the worst was yet to come.

CHAPTER 18

A DIAGNOSIS OF DEPRESSION—MY RESISTANCE

> It is always better to face the truth, no matter how uncomfortable, than to continue coddling a lie.
>
> (Lou Holtz)

The realisation that my marriage was going to end in a divorce was the catalyst for an emotional roller coaster ride for me. I can see now when I look back that I was the one steering myself in that direction. Yes, the penny had dropped but with that came a journey of self-awareness and self-analysis, separate to the issues relating to divorce. It was time I started to look in the mirror in an attempt to workout where my life had gone wrong. In hindsight the timing for my self-awareness and analysis was not so sensible because I was on the verge of being diagnosed with depression.

My depression seemed to creep up on me slowly but looking back there were clear signs that I was heading that way.

I felt in such despair some days that I could not get myself out of bed. I would often cry all day and be so overwhelmed by my emotions. My thoughts seemed chaotic and my brain in turmoil and I can only describe my moods like riding the dips and curves of a roller coaster. It felt like I spent the whole of my time plummeting into the dips and then trying relentlessly to crawl out of them only to find myself slipping back or plummeting into the next dip. It was a constant battle between my brain and my emotions, my rational thinking and my irrational thinking.

I had desperate feelings that some days consumed me and then I would get some relief by going to work and keeping busy until the scenario was repeated.

I recall lying in bed one morning close to lunch time. I woke up in my usual manner and the first thought that popped into my head was of my children getting ready for their day, having breakfast, and heading out the door.

I could generally sense how I was going to cope with the day by the way I had slept and what thoughts were in my mind when I first woke. If I was working I just got up and went, but if it was my day off I would just succumb to my thoughts and stay in bed as long as I wanted.

There was a day that I remember clearly because it caused me a great deal of distress.

This particular day, I dozed most of the morning and when I woke up, I felt frightened and anxious with moisture all over my upper body from sweat. I could recall the cause of my anxiety as a vision that appeared so real to me. I was lying on my back with my face covered in water about 30 cm deep. I was trying to raise my head to get a breath when I felt many arms grabbing at me and pulling me in all directions, wanting me to go this way and that way. I could not choose which way to go but I knew that I had to get some air to breathe, so I started to panic.

It was an overwhelming feeling and my thoughts were muddled so I could not make a decision whilst all these arms were pulling at me. I was not the sort of person that would give up so easily, but I decided I could not fight these arms anymore, so I just relaxed. I had succumbed, knowing that I needed air but just too exhausted anymore to fight for it, and I thought there was little point anyway.

Suddenly the arms let go of me and I pushed my face upwards and gulped a big breath of air. I knew then, that it was time to seek professional help. My emotions were overwhelming and I could no longer deal with them on my own. I spoke that day to a therapist and told her what had happened.

I learnt through my own experience as a child and through my early years of nursing that looking after my emotional well-being was extremely important. It was like personal training for the mind rather than the body, but I knew I had delayed it for too long.

The therapist listened intently and we interpreted the dream as my mind being overwhelmed with everything that was going on. She advised me to heed that message that it is time to take stock, give myself some nurturing, and time to heal myself.

I knew I needed some time to take stock and heal myself, but the concept of giving myself some nurturing was just not in my blood. I was a nurturer who looked after everyone else first and I was last. Nurses are born nurturers, so looking after others comes naturally. I had repeated history by putting the needs of those that surrounded me first and even worse, I felt I put the needs of others in front of the needs of my own children.

CHAPTER 19

A Dark Time—A Place Never Revisited

> Faith is taking the first step even when you don't see the whole staircase
>
> (Martin Luther King)

I had my suspicions that I was becoming more depressed but it took a near suicide attempt before I got the courage to seek proper help. I thought I could manage my self-diagnosed depression on my own. I needed to keep my feelings of wanting to end my life a secret because I felt ashamed. Everything in my personal life seemed chaotic, but my work as a police officer felt like the only stable component of my life. I was losing grip on caring for my children, I was struggling financially, and I felt completely responsible for the position I was in. I gave up on my hope for the future, and I felt like a burden to those around me.

I began the twelve hour night shift as a police officer, my usual cheerful self. The first seven hours, I was kept busy with lots of outstanding work and therefore uneventful. I was working on my own in a shop front station.

In the early hours of the morning around 3 a.m., there was a stark quietness about the place. It was then that tiredness began to set in and with that came the busy thoughts about my crumbling life and my lack of hope that things might get better.

I kept trying to change my feelings of hopelessness, but they just kept pounding back at me like a relentless ocean wave against the rocks. I tried every distraction that I could to just keep those thoughts at bay but nothing worked. I was on that slippery slope towards despair and hopelessness.

I could rationalise that that was where I was headed, but I could not pull back from the steep descent. I sent a text message to a friend that said, 'Are you awake?' I received no answer. I waited for a reply, but it did not come.

I began to sweat and I could feel my heart pumping faster and faster. I was trying to rationalise my thoughts and calm myself. I was alone with my thoughts and that scared me. I looked at my gun in its holster and I quickly looked away. I became restless and walked around the room, I knew where my thoughts were heading and I was fighting to stop them.

The thoughts of my children came into my head but even then my thoughts of hopelessness overpowered the thoughts of my children. The fight with my mind went on for about one hour but seemed like eternity and I was struggling. The proud rational thinking me was losing the battle against my irrational thoughts.

My thoughts continued in a repetitive manner like the wave smashing up against the rocks followed by calmness and then again, the wave smashing up against the rocks and then calmness. The waves started to get faster and faster coming at me relentlessly. My palms started to sweat and my heart was racing. I placed my hand on the handle of my loaded gun and I flicked open the retainer. The thoughts in my head were fighting each other repeatedly arguing back and forth. At the same time I took my gun from its holster and just looked at it. I sat staring at my trigger finger and subconsciously giving my finger instructions to stay away from the trigger whilst I kept fighting the thoughts in my mind. I argued with myself that my life was too hard and difficult. I thought of the burden I felt to my children and the strong feeling that I had failed them by allowing the fairytale to end.

My children were in their home with their father looking after them, so they would be OK. If I did not return home, my life insurance would ease their suffering and their lives would be so much better without me. My thoughts were trying to convince me that I could not endure another day of the mental anguish that I was feeling. I was so overwhelmed with life.

It was at that time I remembered what someone had said to me one day. They told me to picture myself glancing up from my grave and looking into the faces of my children. They told me to imagine the sadness and grief on their faces, the tears in their eyes, and their loss of hope for the future without their mother. I had a flashback from my childhood when my own mother drove away from our house with the intention of driving herself into a tree. I remembered feeling frantic that she would not return alive. I was old enough to remember feeling helpless to do anything other than just wait in the hope she returned alive or was found by police injured or dead.

My thoughts continued to overwhelm me, and I was becoming increasingly confused and disorientated. Suddenly my thoughts were interrupted by the ring of the work telephone. I was the only one there to answer it. I re-holstered my firearm with precision as if I was going about my normal business and then I answered the phone.

It was a simple public enquiry. I went into my professional mode and gave the caller the answer they needed. They thanked me and hung up. When I replaced the handset, I noticed a sense of peace in my head.

The smashing wave had retreated like it had turned in a different direction leaving me in peace for long enough to gain control of my irrational thoughts. The tide had turned and I was still standing. I felt rattled about what had happened but it was close to the time my shift was finishing. I finished the shift in the same cheerful manner that I started and then headed home. I knew I needed to do some serious thinking. I spoke to no one about what had happened. I decided not to put my trust in anyone.

CHAPTER 20

A Shared Story—Brings a Sense of Relief

> No one is useless in this world who lightens the burden of it, to anyone else
>
> (Charles Dickens)

It took me a long time to admit to myself that I was suffering from serious depression but this incident frightened me and I knew that I needed professional help. I had resisted for so long because I wanted to believe that depression just does not happen to people like me.

Once I arrived home, I received a reply from the 'are you awake?' message that I had sent in the early hours of the morning. The reply read 'are you OK?' I sent a message back with a brief account of what had happened although avoided telling the full story. I received a stern phone call from my friend telling me to see my doctor without delay. I knew that he was right.

I went to see my general practitioner and a therapist that same day. I confided in them how I was feeling, but I was not totally honest because I knew that my career would have been finished. I did feel that a heavy weight had been lifted from my shoulders. I have kept the details of that night a secret from everyone, but now I feel it is the right time to speak about it and I also needed to release it from my past.

I had spent so much of my life trying to help everyone else and I started doing this from such an early age when I tried to fix what was happening in my family. It was no wonder that I felt like I had to be superhuman and place unreasonable expectations on myself. After this incident, I realised that no one is superhuman and nor should they try to be. We are who we are and I came to the realisation that I was just a good person trying to do my best. I felt so broken and in need of total repair and thank goodness I was still alive.

I still continued fighting and resisting the diagnosis of depression because I saw it as a weakness in my character and a blemish on my coping mechanisms. I felt ashamed and isolated. I believed that there still remained a stigma attached to depression in some parts of the community, and I did not want to have to deal with that.

I had suffered in silence for too long believing that if my depression was revealed, I would not be able to continue working to the same capacity as I had enjoyed in my new career as a police officer. I felt that I had failed in so many ways in my life already that this was yet another failure.

Initially I did not believe I could tell anyone about my worsening depression because I felt a shadow would be cast over my ability to perform my duties. My emotional stability would be scrutinised and any control I had over my treatment could be taken away from me. I understood the scrutiny because of my nursing background and the nature of policing but I was not ready to subject myself to that. If I did not have my career then I would be lost. Being scheduled under the mental health act was never an option for me. I knew that I had to keep my secret about that night alone with my firearm.

Once I confided in my therapist that I felt depressed, I no longer had to carry the fear and burden of my emotions on my own. I had felt so isolated and lonely in my thoughts amongst a world of friends, family, and colleagues. Most days I felt like I was trapped in the lonely world of misery.

Whilst my pain was invisible, I wanted someone to ask me how I was feeling and I hoped for the day that I felt comfortable to reveal my true feelings. I was not going to volunteer it because I was ashamed and felt that it was a weakness. I also had very little trust in anyone.

One night I had a conversation with a male acquaintance. He was a person that I admired and I looked up to him. We talked about the effect our marriage failures had had on us individually. We lived in separate worlds and our circumstances were very different but we connected straight away. The grief and pain caused by marriage breakdown crosses all boundaries and takes casualties along the way. We both knew the journey we were travelling and where each of us had been, so very few words needed to be said.

This gentleman voiced the distress he felt sometimes with life's difficulties and how hard life was for him. He too experienced times where he wondered to himself if he could get up for another day. I could hear the isolation and loneliness in his voice and the fear associated with those thoughts. He was like me, a rational person who held down a responsible job. He too thought that depression did not affect people like us and thoughts of not wanting to face another day were unspeakable. We were wrong. Anyone of us can have those thoughts, and depression may affect everybody at some point in their lives.

I relayed my personal experience of life after divorce and told him how I had been feeling. I could see the relief on his face. Now he knew that he was not alone in his thoughts. He now realised that his feelings were a normal part of the process when you are experiencing a major life change.

We healed a little piece of each other that night with just a few words. I realised the importance of connecting with someone who understood how I felt. That few moments of conversation was equal to hours of therapy, and some of my preconceived thoughts of depression were lifted. I felt more open to seeking support.

On 2nd September 2009 the BBC news reported that depression looms as a global crisis. The world health organization predicts that within twenty years, more people will be affected by depression than any other health problem. According to WHO, depression will be the biggest health burden on society both economically and sociologically.

This should be a major concern for everyone because if their prediction is correct, then it is likely that each one of us will know someone who is suffering from depression. Therefore it is so important that we ourselves become comfortable talking about depression. Once we feel comfortable about something, we are in a better position to support and encourage those we love to seek help. I believe that as a community, we need to think about mental illness and our own beliefs about it. Chances are that you are ill informed because it is something you might not have needed to think about. What a great opportunity to learn something! You may well need that information to help your best and dearest. If people don't seek help in whatever form, then they cannot receive appropriate treatment or even a cure.

I felt I could not speak out about my depression in fear of losing my credibility within my work environment. I felt personally that there is a lot of ignorance and silence around mental illness. Some people feel ashamed to talk about their illness in fear of being misunderstood, ridiculed, or their personal or professional persona diminished. I ended up being one of them.

I read an article in the Nurses Review Magazine November 2011 with interest recently. The article talked about the Queensland Premier, Anna Bligh's announcement of an $8.5 million, initiative to raise public awareness of the stigma and discrimination associated with mental illness in Queensland. The advertising campaign is called 'change our minds'. The television and newspaper advertisements will urge people to think about the effects their attitudes can have on those with mental illness. I think that any campaign to educate the public on a health matter is a great initiative.

I kept my battle with depression a secret for some of those same reasons and I believed I inhibited my recovery for that very reason. Any attempt to improve the lives of people suffering in silence has to be commended. We need to encourage sufferers to seek support and treatment. During my nursing and policing careers, I have dealt with many people suffering various mental illnesses and to varying degrees of severity. Too many of those were not seeking any help because they believed there was a stigma attached to mental illness. Unfortunately some of those turned up as the suicide cases I investigated.

I am a survivor of depression, but I did it the hard way. I would not wish that on anybody. I did not listen to the advice I was giving my patients or those people I came across during my policing career. I learnt a hard lesson.

CHAPTER 21

WHAT CAN I LEARN—KNOWLEDGE FEEDS US

> Seek out information to empower your healing, YOU will know the answer because it is unique, to who you are.
>
> (Sharon Gardiner)

My therapist had suggested that I continue to see her because I felt overwhelmed with life, but she also voiced that it was equally important that I keep in contact with my general practitioner.

I trusted my GP to guide me in the right direction, but I knew this time I had to be upfront and honest in relation to how I was feeling. Not being honest with her benefited no one, and if I wanted to receive the appropriate treatment for myself, I had no choice.

I confided in her that I had thoughts that I did not want to go on living and that I felt suicide would be an easier option than dealing with everything going wrong in my life. I did not confide in her about the night with my firearm.

She looked at me as if she knew what I was going to say, and she had a relieved look on her face. I interpreted that with a realisation that she sensed how I was feeling, but she was waiting for the words to come out of my own mouth. When I eventually vocalised my thoughts, I no longer felt burdened.

I can honestly say that I was more relieved than her, that my secret was out, and my feeling of isolation was lifted. I had known my GP for some time, and I trusted her to help me, and I was prepared to do whatever it took. After I wiped away the tears, I said in my usual educative manner,

'Right, what is next? I want to know what I need to do.'

I wanted information, education, and some sort of plan. I wanted to beat this and get my life back to normal as soon as possible as long as it was by next week!

No! Unfortunately that was not how it was going to work.

First, I had to accept the fact that I needed medication. This was a significant move forward for me. I was the nurturer, mother, and professional, and I gave out the help not seeking any help myself. I had also taken pride in looking after my health and that included keeping away from regular medications. I was beginning to become a challenging patient for her, but she stood her ground and that was the type of general practitioner I needed.

My GP asked me to return to fill out an online questionnaire in relation to what type of depression I had. She wanted to make sure I got the best treatment for the right diagnosis. I liked this idea immediately because my nursing background taught me to treat each patient's individual needs. I wanted to have information, definitions, reasons, answers, and more importantly a direction forward.

I returned another day and filled out the detailed questionnaire. I believe it was called a mood assessment program or MAP from the Black Dog Institute attached to the Prince of Wales Hospital. When I was given the results, I was not surprised that my personality traits contributed somewhat to my depression. I scored very high in the area of perfectionism (setting high standards), anxious worrying (internalises stress), self-criticism (very tough on myself), interpersonal sensitivity (highlighted by rejection and abandonment). None of these traits surprised me, but what it did highlight to me was that I needed to take a long hard look at myself and it was not going to happen overnight.

These personality traits were just as important for me to rebalance as is the importance of a smoker to change their smoking habits.

I had to change the personality traits that were *not* supportive of my recovery from depression. This was my priority and I called it 'cutting myself some slack'.

I knew a proportion of my personality traits related to some of my experiences as a child coupled with the feeling of rejection in my later adult life. I felt I had failed as a daughter and as a wife and mother, and this resulted in an exacerbated feeling of low self-esteem.

I had placed very high expectations on myself, and just as I got close to reaching an achievement in my life, I would raise the bar higher, never stopping to celebrate. I just kept raising the bar and subconsciously thinking, I have just got to do better, better, better. I had been chasing a moving target all my life. I liken it to walking towards a mirage. I believed the mirage was my answer to all my life's problems and challenges, but the mirage is only an illusion and therefore did not exist. I was chasing something that did not exist. I was a disaster waiting to happen and destined to fall in a heap at some point in my life.

I reluctantly started on medication and my GP checked my general health. I did not respond well to the first medication and this added to my resistance to medication.

My GP reviewed the medication and consequently changed it to something different, which seemed to suit me better. I had no ill effects after that. I made a commitment to myself that I would stay on the medication for as long as the GP thought necessary, and I stuck to it.

I knew that it was going to be a long process to complete recovery, and I was a little annoyed with myself that I had not sort help earlier but in saying that, it was time to stop beating myself up. It was time to start rebuilding the new and improved me.

I learnt to accept medication and I did that by changing my perception of it. I used to subconsciously think that the medication was a treatment for my weakness, which was *not* a productive thought.

I changed my perception of medication to 'a treatment of the temporary chemical imbalance of my brain caused by several life crisis occurring simultaneously'. That sounded much more positive and conducive to my recovery. It may not have been clinically correct, but it suited me.

CHAPTER 22

THE ULTIMATE SACRIFICE—NO PLACE FOR JUDGEMENT

> Always anticipate the best outcome for yourself and others.
> (Leon Nacson)

After my separation, I was struggling to manage a single household, two children, and a new career. I put everything into my policing career because I felt that that was all I had left to financially support myself and my two beautiful children. I was concerned about them being home on their own for a long time because I was gone nearly fourteen hours per day. I changed my work schedule in an attempt to be home earlier for my children, but it meant working an extra day. I had to weigh up what suited us best as a family.

My first night shift in the new department was long and arduous. I was tired before my shift started and I walked the streets of the city for most of the ten-hour shift. I had a lot on my mind and eager to finish, with only one more day until my days off. I completed my shift and started on the journey home in my personal vehicle. It was about 4.45 a.m.

I was driving along a main road and came within three streets of my home when I felt an overwhelming sensation of tiredness, nausea, and sleepiness. I hadn't felt this sensation before so I decided to pull over as quickly as possible, but I needed to find a safe place. I had identified a parking bay in front of a shop only 200 metres up the road. As I approached the parking bay, I must have fallen asleep and was suddenly woken by a loud bang.

I opened my eyes, and my car was heading towards a fence. After striking the fence, the front of my vehicle hit the large tree behind the fence, and I came to an abrupt stop. On impact with the tree, my hand flung up and hit the bottom of the steering wheel. I felt intense pain but the rest of me seemed OK. When I got out of my car, I looked back and saw the support beam of the shop had been snapped in two and the awning was leaning over rather precariously. I realised it was the point of impact with the support post that woke me. My car was badly damaged, but I was alive and more importantly no one else was involved. The only injury I sustained was a small fracture to my left wrist.

I realised almost instantaneously that I had been sent a wake-up call telling me that it was time to re-evaluate the important things in life. I was so thankful to be alive and did not want to think about what might have happened. In just another two hours, the road would have been buzzing with local pedestrians and other cars going about their business.

I stood at the scene in a daze. I was talking to the attending police and firemen when my ex husband arrived. It was then that I was pleased to see a familiar face, but at the same time, I felt awkwardness. Is there an etiquette for ex couples? Do I cry on his shoulder? Do I give him a hug? I did not know. It was then that the realisation came that I was running solo and on my own for the first time in a long time. My only family now were my two children, and they were fast asleep in bed.

I think this accident brought home to me the enormity of separation and the importance we place on attachment to another person. In any case, I had to accept my circumstances and remember why I made the choices I did.

There was a fireman standing next to me and he saw me wipe a tear from my eye. He placed his arm around my shoulder and with a firm squeeze and a reassuring hug, he said, 'It will be OK, mate.'

That was a special moment for me because with that simple gesture from a stranger, I felt that someone cared and reassured me that at least I was alive.

After the initial shock of the accident, I became very anxious about my capabilities in looking after my children. I was in the early stages of separation, a new demanding career, and university studies to complete. I still had to manage the daily activities of my children but now without a car.

I was very lucky to have only sustained a broken wrist; however, this injury was enough to take me away from my full policing duties. I was very well supported by my police colleagues, and my boss was wonderful. I had his full support and that allowed me to continue all the professional and university requirements to complete my probationary year. It was a challenge for me, being out of action for at least six weeks. I was blessed that the other school mums helped with my children and I would be able to borrow a car for some of the time.

I was struggling to keep my head above water in every aspect of my life, and I did not want my children to see their mother broken and unable to cope. I did not want to subject them to an emotionally unstable environment as I had been subjected to as a child. My children's welfare was the most important thing to me.

Our divorce was thrust upon them, and they had no say or choice in the matter. I did not want my children to remember their childhood as a time of instability and I knew in myself that I was finding it harder and harder to provide them with the stability that they should expect.

Having some time away from my regular policing duties gave me a chance to take a breath and reevaluate life. The pain and inconvenience of a broken wrist reminded me, not only of my accident, but also the wakeup call it sent.

I thought carefully about what was best for my children and in doing that, I remembered my own childhood and the chaos that came with it.

I made the difficult decision to step back from my children's lives, but I made it to ensure they would be taken care of and I felt at the time the better person to do that was their own father. In my heart, the decision was very difficult, but in my brain, I could find no better solution. They were my number one priority, and I recognised that taking the time away from my children would give them back a better and happier mother. I was exhausted and on an emotional roller coaster. I was mentally unstable and suffering depression and I did not want my kids to see that. They were so innocent and deserved the best start to life.

My children loved their father and he loved them more. I knew that he could provide them with a secure and stable environment, and he was also a good man. I knew that they would get the love that they needed but most of all; their lives would not be too disrupted.

The decision to have children was a huge commitment to me. I took the responsibility of raising them very seriously. I could not think that my choice to step back from their care was a bad one. I did it for them.

I knew that living away from my children was going to be difficult. I would miss every little bit of them. I did not see any other way. I had to protect them at any cost.

I had made a difficult decision in the past to protect my children so I was fortunate to be able to reflect back on that. I looked back on the time

I decided to shield my children from the instability of my own family. I kept my children away from my mother and father because I could not guarantee that they would be spared the heartache that I was still experiencing as an adult. My daughter at one point said to me, 'Mum, I think you have given your family more than enough chances. It's time to move on'.

I thought that she was so wise and I admired the way she could see clarity in something that was so foggy for me. I have protected my children from their grandparents all their lives. It has been over twenty years since my daughter has seen her grandparents and my son has never seen them.

I had to make that decision to keep them safe. I did not believe that they would be in danger in a physical sense. I was more concerned about the emotional scars. It did not matter to me whether that was the reality, what mattered to me was that they were not going to suffer the way I did. Whether I believed that would happen or not, I was not willing to take the chance. My children are too precious to me to take a risk.

CHAPTER 23

THE POLICE FAMILY—A SPECIAL BOND

> The service we render others is the rent we pay for our room on earth.
>
> (Wilfred Grenfell)

One thing that depression taught me was that it can happen as result of some critical event in your life either internally or externally no matter how much support or preparation for the event. My separation was the result of me wanting to find happiness and a new direction in my life. The crises that occurred one by one during that time, I believe I needed to experience because there were lessons for me to learn from all of them.

When my marriage ended, I felt stripped bare of everything that meant anything to me. I had been a wife and mother for seventeen years and that was all I thought I needed and wanted. The change for me was a massive one and like a raindrop hitting a pond it started one big ripple effect, crossing paths with all areas of my life.

The changes reminded me of a time when my daughter was little and she loved to dress up. She would drape strings of pearls and beads around her neck, then put on a pair of my shoes, and finish the outfit with that special handbag. She would walk around so proudly looking very important and sophisticated.

I remember on one occasion that the string holding some pearls broke and caused the pearls to drop all over the floor, going in every direction. Where the pearls landed was unpredictable and as the pearls were rolling around, I would make that last minute grab to try and salvage any pearls left on the string. It was upsetting for my daughter but we could work together to collect them and then put the necklace back together. If I were to make a comparison of my life after separation to those scattering pearls, then you can imagine the enormity of what was ahead for me.

If the string of pearls represented my life in its neat and tidy bundle and each pearl represented a special part of that life, then the ripple effect would be immeasurable. My life was essentially on the floor spread in all directions. Some pearls just lay there waiting to be found easily and some were hidden in hard to get places. I imagine myself slowly and carefully picking them up one by one and putting them into a bag.

I could look at the bag and think to myself 'where would I start? And who would be there to give me some direction or help me?' I could think of no one. I felt I was alone and isolated with my shattered life, represented by my bag of loose pearls and a broken string. A portion of those pearls could be sorted easily because they represented unimportant stuff. Another portion could be put aside till later because they represented possessions and material things. What was left in the bag represented my shattered soul. The pearls represented the grief and loss associated with separation and the crumbling of a relationship and a family unit. If I imagined myself looking at those pearls with an ocean of tears running down my cheeks, I would be thinking. Which shattered piece of me needs attention first, but then again who is me anyway? Which one of those pearls represents me? I did not know anymore. I had lost myself.

My journey had to have a clear beginning and that needed to begin with finding and nurturing the pearl that existed in me when I was born. The person I used to know as myself was nowhere to be found. I needed to carefully pick up each pearl and nurture it back onto the string. The timing of that nurturing was to be determined by the journey ahead. There was no compass, no timetable, and no deadline.

The thought of soul-searching and healing the hurt was far too overwhelming in the early stages of my separation, so I clung to my new career as a police officer like it was all I had. I felt my new career gave me some direction in life at a time that my internal compass was spinning crazily amongst a haze of unknowns.

I had achieved my dream, and I had also become a respected member of the NSW Police among my colleagues and peers. I felt proud of what I had achieved, and I had earned the position out of my own drive and determination. I put all my efforts into my job, knowing that my life on the other hand was not going to be so easy. My job as a police officer was one of those pearls that had to take priority. I needed to financially support myself.

I worked in the city environment, and as we know from the many media reports that the city of Sydney never sleeps, this new life was exciting for me, but at the same time was overshadowed by sadness because I could not enjoy my success within my family unit. I was, however, amongst the most wonderful team of colleagues that really genuinely cared for me. I believe working as a police officer was so much more intense than working as an emergency nurse. My police colleagues used to laugh at me when I would make that comment because they viewed nursing as quite the opposite. I agree that emergency nursing was very hard work, but I had been doing it for so long that it was rather mundane for me. Whilst working as an emergency nurse, the shift was always busy, and we ran for a solid eight hours sometimes not even stopping to drink, eat, or wee. At the end of the shift, I went home and never gave the job much thought.

My time as a police officer was very different. I had a huge workload that just did not stop after the twelve-hour shift. I was always behind in my paperwork and trying to cope with the many briefs of evidence for court matters was difficult. I knew I was very capable but I was new to that side of work, and I spent quite a bit of my own personal time sweating over my work. It was just something that most of us did because we had deadlines, and when you are working in a busy station, you are constantly answerable to the police radio.

The level of stress was high, but the camaraderie was something that I will treasure for a long time. The high stress of the four twelve-hour shifts brought a sigh of relief at the end of the week and the beginning of our days off.

CHAPTER 24

A Trip to Self Discovery—Where Did I Go

> Make the most of yourself because that is all there is of you.
> (Ralph Waldo Emerson)

To let off steam at the end of the gruelling week, our team often went for drinks. This was the first time for me that I would be sitting in a pub at eight in the morning and having a full breakfast washed down with a beer. The laughter was plentiful and the week's gruelling schedule would be off loaded as if we did not have a care in the world. We all knew, though, that on our return after days off, our work would be waiting for us.

I enjoyed these let-off-steam sessions thoroughly, and considering that I was in most cases the oldest one there, I used to hold-up pretty well against the younger ones. One session I recall went all day. I finished work at 7.30 a.m. and headed home around 9.30 p.m. that night. I felt part of something really special, and I had not felt part of something special for a long time. Of course my children have been the most beautiful people that have come into my life and I cherish them, but as for me as a person, I had not felt special or wanted for such a long time.

The nights or days out among my police colleagues were so much fun because we just released all the stresses of the week, and we could laugh about anything in life. I had started the habit of drinking a bit too much on some of the nights out that we went on, but when I say too much, I was a rather cheap drunk with my limit of about three glasses of wine. I was living close to the city and could easily walk home or catch a taxi.

One time, I attended a colleague's anniversary of thirty years in the job. It was a celebration that he deserved and we wanted to share this time with him. At the end of the dinner, when most people had gone home, we went on to celebrate in one of the popular city drinking holes. I was quite intoxicated by this stage and I was having difficulty walking a zigzag line, let alone a straight line. There was about six of us at that time, and the security man standing at the door of the pub had watched us walk across the road. We were hoping he would let us enter. I was not surprised that he refused my entry due to my level of intoxication, but my colleague popped up and said, 'She has only had two glasses of wine.'

I said, 'Bullshit, you're lying. I have had about two bottles not two glasses', and I burst out laughing.

At that time, everyone started to laugh including the door security and the line of people waiting to get in. I was therefore in the next taxi on my way home.

I had at that time many gay friends, and I was sharing a unit within walking distance of Oxford Street, Darlinghurst. I started to spend a lot of time in Oxford Street, which was great fun. I loved dancing and I would be in the clubs all night long dancing myself silly. Then at around seven in the morning, I would do what was commonly known as the 'walk of shame' whilst heading for the first taxi. I felt very safe in this environment and because I was in a vulnerable state emotionally, it was perfect for me to let my hair down and so I did.

One year, I found myself at the sleaze ball. It is a big dance party celebrating gay life and is held once per year. I thought it would be some fun, so I went with several of my gay friends and literally had one of the best times I had had for ages. I can only say that for someone who was married for seventeen years and was living the life of a wife and mother, I was now truly in my element. I felt I was back in my early teen life being twenty once again with a carefree spirit to match.

I was really taken aback by the hot bodies that surrounded me at this event I had not seen anything like it in one place in my lifetime. The hotties were in every direction (both guys and girls). I would have been happy to stay in the corner just watching them walk past. I was in party heaven, and I really enjoyed the company of all involved because everyone was in for some fun and frivolity. This was quite different from the George Street Sydney strip where I worked dealing with alcohol-related issues night after night. During the middle of the night, it became quite hot in the venue (temperature wise), and we were all dancing as one big mass of people. Most of the people had their shirts off and looked somewhat more comfortable than me. I thought what a good idea, so I grabbed the neck of my top and pulled it out in front of me. I checked out the condition and look of the bra I was wearing. Once I realised it was pretty darn sexy and in tip-top shape, I whipped off my top. I felt safe and comfortable amongst everyone, and dancing with bra only, I felt completely liberated and rather feminine. I felt that I could relax without judgement and just enjoy feeling good because I was having a great time. My nights out amongst the gay community were some of the most carefree and uninhibited nights that I had had for a long time.

I had been living with a female for about eight months at that time, and she was going through similar times to me. She was not a police officer but a mutual friend. I got out of my part of the lease early for several of my own personal reasons but basically because I wanted to be elsewhere. It was a period of great instability for me and committing to anything long term was not a good idea. We enjoyed each other's company though, especially when we went out.

One night, we were out together and a young man must have thought we were together as female partners. He said that he would like to see two women kiss, so we looked at each other and we went for it. Next thing, we were kissing each other on the lips, and the kiss seemed to last for some time. I can remember how unbelievably soft her lips were. We both thought it was a funny thing to ask two women so we just had to oblige. When the kiss was over, we just went back to enjoying the night. We didn't discuss the kiss as it was just a moment in time where we felt free spirited and carefree. We were free of the men in our lives, and we were free spirits discovering ourselves again. It was a beautiful moment.

I have always been clear of my sexuality but this moment felt right for the time and I just happened to have many gay friends whose company I enjoyed immensely. It was interesting to hear the 'work gossip'. They had me pinned as 'a mid-forties divorcee, lost and swapping sides'. I thought that was funny because they were so far from the truth. I let them think what they wanted. I laugh every time I hear K. Perry's song called I kissed a girl. One day I found myself singing it whilst having a chuckle to myself.

I believe there is something to be said about being free spirited and for me that meant doing what pleased me and what I felt was right at the time. I have no regrets. I was busy finding myself again because I did not know who I was anymore. I felt like I had lived a different life to what I may have been meant to.

I remained among my friends in the gay community for some years, and I travelled overseas with one particular gay friend. Our first night in Los Angeles started with a tasty American dinner full of chips and ketchup and followed up by drinks at the local club with some newly acquired friends. I was really intent on letting my hair down; however, I was not used to the American way of service of alcohol compared to Australia. This led me to drinking like a maniac. I was drinking very strong cocktails packed with glazed cherries soaked in more alcohol. The clubs in this Los Angeles area closed up around 2 a.m., but there did not seem to be any restrictions on how many drinks they served you.

In Sydney, the clubs stay open all night but restrict the amount of alcohol you can consume. It was a heavy drinking session waiting to happen! I was amongst newly acquired friends, so it turned out I did not buy one drink that night. I had completely lost count but what the heck I came without a car.

After several hours of heavy drinking, we left the club and stopped in at a pizza place on the way home. I needed to go to the bathroom and I was pointed the direction by a friend. There were two doors and I was not sure which was the door to the ladies, so I just opened the first one and ended up outside behind the pizza place in a very dark back alley.

I tried to orientate myself but by this stage, I was completely legless and the two doors had turned to four. I turned around and stumbled into the side of a large trash can. I went for a dive into the ground, sliding along my left shoulder. This resulted in a piece of skin being sheared off my shoulder like someone had taken a vegetable grater to it. The next thing to hit the ground was my head and just to top it off, I hit it face first, leaving me with a black and bruised eye. I lay there on the ground thinking to myself 'this is not good, no one knows where I am. I have no phone numbers and I am legless'. Then followed that was an 'I have been really naughty chuckle' signifying that I knew I was in big trouble from my friends. I looked down, and my top was wide open with my black bra showing to the moon when I heard deep voices. I looked up and saw two men looking down at me. They started to ask me what happened and it was then that I tried to tell them. Not only did I have alcohol induced slurred speech, but they could also not understand my Aussie accent.

These two lovely gentlemen had found me in a sorry state, and they were so caring and patient with me. Thank goodness, I was too drunk to be embarrassed.

I handed them my phone, and they were able to find a phone number of one of my newly acquainted friends. Soon after, my friends came running and saw me in my sorry state. Boy, was I in trouble! They got me to my feet and stood either side of me. We headed straight for a taxi where the three of us headed back to the motel. I was not a pretty sight and I am glad that I live on the other side of the world. The worst was to come when I vomited in the driveway of our five-star motel on the first night of our five-night stay. I was rather embarrassed but unfortunately too intoxicated to care. This was not my proudest moment.

After a long process getting cleaned up and changed, I got into bed feeling sore and sorry for myself. My friends had attended to my shoulder as best they could, and I felt no pain. They laid out a towel over the sheet to protect the bed from my bleeding shoulder.

I woke up during the night feeling rather confused, so I attempted to reorientate myself to where I was. At that time I looked over my right shoulder and I saw my two male friends asleep in the next bed. I tried to determine if I was sober or still drunk and if I was actually seeing what I was looking at (or still seeing double) so I took another look. It was then that I took a double take, lifting my painful head off the pillows to get a closer look and then I chuckled to myself and thought how my life had changed. I was once a wife and mother with two professional careers, heavily involved in my children's school as president of the Mothers club and canteen helper. Not forgetting that I was aged forty-five!.

I laughed to myself and thought 'Oh my goodness, . . . my life is so different. Was that life I remember as a wife and mother of two children real? And if so, how the hell did I get to this point in my life? What happened that I am in a motel room looking across at my two male friends in the same bed and I am laying here with a painful eye and a chunk of skin off my shoulder?'

I am a responsible, hard-working, loving individual who holds down a great career. Am I still that person? Where was my life heading after this? It was surreal for a moment but then I just relaxed and thought of the excitement of not knowing what was next. Best of all, I had no one to answer to other than a not so amused friend but hey, he was going to get over it. I felt like I had spent my whole life so regimented and just doing everything to please everyone else. I felt I had to do what was deemed right by the fairytale. Well, now look at me, stuff what everyone thinks. I had fun.

I remember myself as a young person or teenager. I used to have so much fun and loved to laugh at everything. I wanted to recapture those fun times. I was away from Australia, away from the thoughts of separation and the pain that came with those thoughts. This time was about me for a change. I just hoped I was going to survive. The trip I had was so fantastic and I felt carefree, uninhibited and relaxed.

CHAPTER 25

THE PAIN BEHIND THE SMILE—MY SECRET

> Sometimes when I say, 'I'm OK. I want someone to look me in the eyes. Hug me tight and say, 'I know, you are not'.
>
> (Unknown)

I returned back to my life as a police officer and back to the grind of the long days but in saying that, I thrived on it. I loved every minute of the job. This was me now. I was no longer a full-time mother, a housewife, a nurse, or school mum. It seemed that I had a new identity and this brought lots of adjustments both good and bad.

I was living my dream of being a police officer, but at the same time in the back of my mind, my fairy tale dream was over. I woke up every morning with my children in my thoughts rather than them at the end of my bed telling me they want breakfast.

I appeared to everyone to have a wonderful new exciting life on the outside, but I did not feel like that on the inside. On the inside, I missed my children terribly and I felt guilty for leaving them. I felt a failure as a daughter, a failure as a wife, and a failure as a mother to my children. These thoughts were always present while I still had to deal with the relentless crashing wave of depression that would lap at my feet. Not forgetting the emotional roller coaster ride that I endured day in and day out. Just as I crawled my way to the top of the incline, I knew that I would either hover on the top for a while or go straight down for the next bit of emotional chaos. I had no control over the veracity or length of the roller coaster journey and no control of that relentless lapping wave.

It was a day by day scenario and I just rode it and went wherever I was taken.

In amongst the social events celebrated with my policing colleagues, I would try and see my children as often as possible.

In the few years after my marriage split, I had free and open access to my children in the house they shared with their father and of course our golden retriever. It was not unusual that I just chilled out with my children in the house. Some days their father would return home and we would all have a chat about the day and I would leave when it suited.

This period of time in my life brought some normality to the situation, and I still felt very much a parent of my two children. I know it was difficult for all involved and there are always issues with separation and divorce, but we all just did the best we could at the time. The children were the most important people to both of us.

It came time that my children's lives would be blended into a new family life. After the purchase by their father of a new family home, my children were going to live there with him and his new partner and our dog. My ex husband created a good home for our children, and they were set up with all the comforts that they needed and I was pleased that they were settled in the area close to their friends. After a short time, I was able to be given a tour of their bedrooms and I appreciated that. After a brisk shake of their father's new partner's hand, I left my children to begin the next phase in their lives.

The thought of them living there gave me a lump in my throat every time. When that happened, I just had to remind myself about the choices I had made and why. That was the simple part because I made my choices to give them a better life than I could provide.

No matter how many times I reminded myself of the reasons I made the choices I did, it was still incredibly hard, painful, and heart wrenching. I needed all the strength I could muster when I returned to the house usually for the purpose of taking them somewhere or bringing them home. I found myself falling into a pattern of avoidance. I did not want to avoid seeing my children but I did want to avoid the scenario of driving up that driveway and the reminder that my children were inside the house being cared for within a new family. I could not help but to think that I had been replaced. It seemed to me like one minute we were married and the next I had been completely forgotten. A little bit dramatic I know but that is how I was feeling.

The experience of having to visit my children gave me an understanding of some of the frustrations of the many fathers who are living away from their children. The pain and anguish they must endure when they have limited access to their children must be extremely difficult. I did not have limited access to my children in a visitation sense but just in a location sense. I enjoyed seeing my children, but the emotional burden that was created by the visual reminder that they shared a different family life was sometimes unbearable. I only knew myself as a mother to my children and I felt that I was no longer part of that. I was no longer providing those special lunches with the sailboat sandwiches, the bed time stories with my playful antics, organising their bags, and daily pickup and drop off timetable. I lost contact with the school mums, became unknown to my son's friends, and was no longer able to hear the constant chatter of my daughter's daily experiences.

I was now just a police officer, living my dream not knowing what each day may bring. Everything was new and unfamiliar, but my soul continued to yearn to be the mother that I had been for so long. No one around me at that time seemed to understand what I was feeling because in reality, I was the creator of my destiny and I had made my own choices. I was the one who pursued entry into the police service, I wanted out of my marriage, and it was my decision to live away from my children. How could anyone try to understand when I did not understand myself? My dream felt empty.

The demands of my career made it easy for me to push the pain away and the camaraderie sheltered me in some way from having to bear it. I was surrounded by my colleagues who knew the fragility of life, the burden of emotional struggles, and we could all reconcile in the fact that as one day ends, another will come.

I went to a night out with my work team, and later in the night, I saw my sergeant sitting on a bar stool, gazing into nowhere. I went and sat with him and he told me of the strain he felt of not seeing his children after separation. He told me of his love for them and how he missed them so much and felt frustrated that he could not see them when he wanted to. I supported him that night as we all supported each other. I could relate to his sadness and I placed my hand on his shoulder in an attempt to comfort him knowing that it was only a small gesture in amongst a mountain of grief.

It was only a few weeks later that he came to talk to me about a trip he had planned. He was taking his children on a holiday and his eyes lit up with excitement when he told me. He was full of enthusiasm and was counting the days until it was time to leave. I was thrilled and excited for him and could see that he had a new lease on life. It was wonderful to witness.

CHAPTER 26

ALWAYS THEIR MOTHER—ALWAYS HER CHILDREN

> A mother's love for her child is like nothing else in the world. It knows no law, no pity; it dares all things and crushes down remorselessly, all that stands in its path.
>
> (Agatha Christie)

My sergeant's story got me thinking about my own children and it was then that I decided to take my children away with me. I had just planned to take a holiday and had a flexible itinerary. As they grew up, we had often spoken about going to Disneyland, so it made sense that we headed that way. A short time later, I was off to Los Angeles with my two children for a ten day holiday.

Due to time constraints with their study, they were going to fly home at the end of the ten days and then I would continue my trip to New York and then San Francisco.

There was excitement in the air as we travelled, and I could not wait to have my children in my life, just the three of us for ten days.

It was about two days into the trip that I realised that I was still their mother. I had felt that I had been replaced by someone else and I had little control over anything to do with them. Those sweet little children that I nursed as babies were growing up without me in their everyday lives. It was heart wrenching.

I wanted to remember the special moments whilst in our hotel together so when I woke up in the middle of the night, I would just sit and look at my children sleeping in their beds. They were in their pyjamas cuddling in the warmth with their heads laid gently on their pillows. I would take one last look and then lay my head down on my own pillow and with a smile on my face I would drift off to sleep with thoughts of gratitude that I had this special time with them.

What was I thinking when I made those choices? Did I not realise that I was going to be heartbroken? Did I not think that I was going to miss seeing them take every breath of life?

Here we were in the small hotel room sleeping in the same room, laughing and joking. Talking about the excitement of the day like nothing had changed since they were little. I remember looking at their faces and realising that I was their mum and always will be. There is no replacement for a mother and no one can replace me as a person either. It was rather silly for me to think that in any case.

The holiday went so well and every minute with my children was so precious to me. I saw them off at the Los Angeles airport for their journey home with their suitcases full of purchases and I waved them goodbye knowing that I was their mum again. It was only the geography that had changed.

After I waved them goodbye, I went on to New Jersey to spend some time with my good friend Renata. She was only a short train ride away from New York City. I had visited New York once before on a quick visit so I was very excited to return. We had a wonderful time together and visited many attractions. I spent some days in Manhatten by myself just chilling out and doing my own thing.

I was moved by the 911 tragedy and spent a lot of time looking over the many memorial sights trying to imagine how the city recovered from such a terrible event. As a police officer, I felt saddened to know that many people lost their lives and did not return home to their families. That is always something that is on the minds of police officers around the world when leaving their families in the morning and not being able to say 100 per cent that they will return.

One beautiful sunny morning, I caught the ferry over to see the Statue of Liberty. The statue depicts a woman draped in robes with an outstretched arm that holds a torch. To me, the significance was that she was raising her arm in triumph like she had broken through or reached her destination.

The statue represents 'Libertas' who is the 'roman goddess' of freedom'

I sat for hours and just looked at the sheer beauty and elegance of this statue. I felt connected in some ways but knew that my journey to freedom was continuing. I visualised that one day I could raise my arm and feel a sense of freedom and celebration of a journey travelled. I kept a postcard of the Statue of Liberty on my wall at home and I dreamt one day I will return to see this roman goddess when I feel, I myself am liberated.

My trip to America with my children was such a reassuring experience for me as a mother. The time we shared together has a special place in my heart and I felt at peace. The pearl that represented that part of my life had been nurtured back on to the string. When my holiday ended, it was inevitable that I must return home and back to the reality of work and life away from my children.

On arrival back at work, I felt accomplished in my mission to restore my belief that I was still the mother of my children and confidant that I was slowly starting to restring my pearls.

CHAPTER 27

FEELING LIKE A MILLION DOLLARS—
AN UNFAMILIAR FEELING

> If you don't love yourself, nobody else will. Not only that—you won't be good at loving anyone else. Loving starts with the self.
>
> (Dr Wayne W. Dyer)

I returned to everyday life when my attention was caught by a man who I met within two days of arriving home. I thought he was incredibly handsome, fit-looking, and immaculate in his appearance. I spoke to him for a short period and we established very quickly that we had a lot of common ground. In such a short conversation, we discovered that we shared the same star sign, age, and had two children each the same age. We were both single. I was already divorced and he was separated. I was taken by this man's compassion and friendliness. The ease of conversation, his warmth, and smile were the things that struck me the most.

Did I believe he would be interested in me?

Absolutely not, I straight away put him right up there out of my league as I had often done. I did not believe that someone like that could be interested in me. There was something about him though, that I just could not let go of and I thought 'Oh, what the heck have I got to lose, so I asked him to have a coffee with me'.

Well, knock me down dead, he accepted my invitation. Due to heavy work commitment it took sometime before we could arrange a convenient time. We eventually caught up with dinner at my place instead. I was excited but so nervous at the same time. No one had paid me this attention for longer than I could remember, and I found it hard to believe I was the subject of that attention. I had two conflicting thoughts that night in my head, one was that I had a handsome man in my kitchen and the other was that he was there visiting me. I could not connect the thoughts easily and I was not really sure why. I was feeling really happy and comfortable, but at the same time full of self-doubt and fear. I think the self-doubt came from my ongoing feeling of being undeserving, and the fear came from my experience of relationships and rejection.

When I eventually relaxed the thoughts inside my brain, with a glass of nice wine, we started to talk and never drew breath. Well, I talked continuously as I always do and he listened intently, occasionally contributing so articulately with his own story. We spoke about anything and everything and connected so easily like we had known each other for a long time.

The night just got better and better and I felt relaxed about myself. I felt I could be myself, just me and he was accepting of just me. We spent a wonderful night together where he cuddled me in his arms for what seemed like hours. I felt cared for and feminine. These feelings had been buried deep in a closet with layers of cobwebs for a very long time and I never thought anyone could ever open that closet again.

It is moments like that when you realise that you can be married for many years but still feel so alone. This connection was the type of intimacy that I had been craving for most of my life and I felt starved and deprived of it. This night I had allowed myself to be accepting of his affection without fear of the rejection that I had become accustomed to.

After he left I felt alive again. I mean really alive. I felt in some way that I had reclaimed a small part of my true self. I had realised I had put my needs and desires aside for others and that had taken me far away from who I was inside.

I started to think '*Wow,* someone does desire me and is attracted to me.' This was a whole new concept for me. I felt warmth inside and a sense of relief that a part of me had returned.

In the small time that we spent together I could not recall feeling the same way for many years. This was a new experience for me, and I was learning some good lessons about how I perceived myself. I also started to recognise my thought patterns, and that I had viewed the difficulties in my marriage as just something that I should accept and now I began to see it differently. I believed that marriage was about the love of each other and the connecting of the souls through intimacy, but my experience was so different.

I was learning another important lesson about my thought processes. I had accepted the situation within my marriage and told myself that I was undesirable because that is how I felt. It was not until I met this man who showed interest in me that I realised my negative view of myself. This was a major awakening for me because I had expected others to make me feel good about myself.

There were two more times that we spent talking and listening to each other. I found those times to be so incredibly refreshing to me. I was at a time in my journey when my optimism or belief that something wonderful would return to my life was deeply buried. I tried hard to keep my feet on the ground because I could still not believe this man could be interested in me. I was feeling on top of the world when I met him for lunch. It was just as wonderful and for the rest of the day, I was feeling like a million dollars. I let myself enjoy the moment, but I was aware I had this feeling of fear in the back of my mind. It was telling me to be cautious and protect myself because rejection may come. That little voice of self-doubt was spinning the negative messages around my brain like a pendulum, swinging unobtrusively. Just to keep me reminded that I was undeserving of anything that remotely resembled happiness. I could though every now and then, hear a little weak voice inside me say 'enjoy it' and go with the flow.

On the fourth occasion, I sensed something was not right but I talked myself into thinking that I had already prepared myself for failure so would not be upset. As I sat there and listened to him talk about his need to make a further attempt to reconcile his marriage, I was therefore already familiar with my feelings. I had been there before, but this time was different because I could understand his open communication of the reasons he had to make that choice. I had not been given the same privilege of openness previously, and I was reassured in some way that his reasons for bringing something wonderful to a halt were valid and sincere.

My feeling like a million dollars soon deflated to what resembled a few loose coins. The romance was short-lived and wonderful, but the lessons I learnt from that experience helped me to unravel some habitual negative messages I had been hearing for so long. I was of course sad that I was not going to see this man again, but I believed he had done the best thing for both of us.

The few times we met have a special place in my memory and I believe that if it was meant to be then our paths may cross again one day.

I could now start to rebuild my feelings of self-worth, knowing that the messages from the past no longer served me and it was time to slowly release them. I had essentially formed relationships with people in my past with the overwhelming need to gain their acceptance and approval in order for me to love and approve of myself.

The fact that a man could come into my life for such a short time and wake-up me up to this notion was very liberating for me. The only person I need to seek approval from is me. This man thought I was a beautiful and strong woman, and I thank him for reflecting back to me who I really am. I take back my power and I take it back now. I have rediscovered my true self, and I am proud of who I have become.

It sounds like a happy ending (I laugh out loud) but that was not so. I had even more lessons to learn and I knew for me I was going to continue to learn the hard way.

CHAPTER 28

PEOPLE WORSE OFF—THEY ARE EVERYWHERE

> Our problems seem enormous until you hear the plight of others and you realise it is time to put yours into perspective.
> (Sharon Gardiner)

To complicate matters around this time, I was hit hard emotionally by the sudden death of my brother and then the terminal cancer diagnosis of a close friend.

After the shock of hearing that news, I began to think a little bit differently about what I needed to do to heal myself. I could not let my feeling of grief for two important people in my life slow my progress. I needed to prepare myself for the challenges ahead. The best way I knew how to prepare myself was to educate myself further than what I had already done.

I recognised that I was not capable of giving my friend any parts of myself at a time when she was in great need. I knew that my other friends within our group would make sure that she was cared for. I spoke with her as often as I could. The concept of pulling back was difficult for me because healing and nurturing came naturally to me, but I had to make a conscious decision to put myself first this time.

On the other hand, her diagnosis and eventual death as well as my brother's death made me feel that my situation was insignificant. Looking in from the outside I could see that was a valid point, but I was not mentally strong enough to see it that way. My situation was real to me, and therefore I had to concentrate on moving myself forward because no one else could do it for me.

Stepping back was a major change for me, but I knew that it was my only choice if I wanted to recover. I had to also remember that I had sacrificed caring for my children to help my recovery, and I owed it to them to prioritise myself.

I got a lot of personal satisfaction from helping others, and I chose two careers that reinforced that, but I do very poorly when it comes to nurturing myself. This personality trait was definitely a contributing factor to my depression. My depression struck when I had nothing left to give of myself. I was like an empty hot air balloon completely deflated and wilted on the ground. I had nothing left to give anyone. I was empty and in need of reinflating *but* it was going to have to be done in stages and I was only just beginning.

I am a believer in self-education and therefore a lover of self-help books, so in my own search for education, I started in the self-help section of the local book store.

With the results of my depression questionnaire in my mind, I found a book about stress. After all, the results indicated that my personality was a contributing factor to my depression.

My therapist had raised concerns about my stress levels on numerous occasions so I thought a book about stress was a good place to start. In her years of experience as a therapist and a nursing background, she had seen many people get sick for reasons she believed directly resulted from stress. I knew that my friend who died of cancer had suffered long term stress for years before her illness and that scared me.

I picked up a book and inside I saw a stress rating scale. The scale was created by T. Holmes and R. Rahe in 1967 and they called it, Holmes and Rahe stress scale.

The scale measures the amount of stress you have experienced in the preceding twelve months. When you complete the scale, your scores are added up.

The scale is meant to be used as a guide only, but when I looked at it and then added up my score to be well over the highest level of 300, I felt relieved. I wanted to yell out aloud, 'Someone has finally validated my emotional state'

I thought I was going crazy because I perceived everyone around me as dealing well with their stress, yet I felt I was drowning. I could not wait to show this to my therapist because it was something tangible. I had somewhere to start. I wanted to reduce my stress score by working on certain elements that I had control over. I felt I was regaining some control over my situation and that was a definite move forward. I needed to see some progress in my recovery because it gave me hope and knowledge that I was heading in the right direction.

I continued to educate myself as much as possible, and I reiterated what I was learning with my therapist just to make sure I was on the right path. I had good days and bad days in relation to my ability to concentrate and absorb information so I chose short easy snippets of information. I liked books from Australian authors or reputable well known overseas authors. I chose a wide variety of topics initially and then as my mental focus improved, I concentrated on what material I felt was applicable to my situation.

The most difficult thing I found whilst being depressed was that the world did not stop for me. The business of life continued around me, and I had to work and function like everyone else, even on the days I did not want to get out of bed. I had no choice but to survive as hard as it was. I never had another moment like that night where I saw my firearm as a way out of life. I thankfully got help and woke up to the fact that my children needed me in their life.

CHAPTER 29

LIFE IS PRECIOUS—GONE AT FIFTY

> There will never be another now—I'll make the most of today.
> There will never be another me—I'll make the most of myself.
> R.H. Schuller

My brother taught me so many things about life.

After those early years with him, we went on different paths when I started nursing and began living in the nurse's home. My brother was sad when he realised we had to move out of our unit, but I was excited at the prospect of starting a nursing career. My brother found love and eventually married but this was not lasting. He appeared lost in his own world of relationships, but I did not really understand what issues he was experiencing. I sensed that he had a low self-esteem because his actions mirrored mine in some ways.

My brother was having difficulty with his relationship with my mother and later when I was getting married; my brother did not attend my wedding. He told me that he did not want to face my mother. I felt sad that he was not going to be with me on the day, but he could not find it in himself to attend. I was disappointed, but I understood his reasons.

I saw my brother as often as I could, but after sometime, we lost contact. I withdrew from my family at some point in the later years, and it was then that my brother suffered a tragedy with the death of a workmate. It was a tragic accident and my brother blamed himself. I was not there to help him through the trauma but found out years later. By this time, he had moved to America and began a new relationship. I heard that he had begun to rebuild his life and was truly happy for the first time in his life. I can't recall a time that my brother and I ever spoke a bad word to each other but rather our lives just drifted us apart. Among the fond memories of the time I had with my brother, I never took the time out to flick off an email to say 'How you doing?'

Tragically, his happiness was to be short-lived because he died suddenly leaving a grieving wife behind. He was only fifty, and his death not only rocked me because of his age, but also because I had no contact with him for almost ten years. I have never had so much regret that it had been so long since I told my brother that I loved him. I was in Manila at the time, and I could not make it to America but my thoughts were with him in his dying days.

It was his sudden death that lead me to look closer into how I lived my life and what changes I needed to make to improve it. His death left me a legacy. I was about to turn fifty, and I had decided that I was not going to continue along my current path in life where what I did in my future was a reflection of what happened in my past.

I felt it was time that I should start to speak out and communicate my feelings to others. I wanted to be heard. I was slowly peeling away the layers of my past, but I realised that I needed to do more because life is precious and can be taken away from us without warning. I thank my brother because in his life, he helped me and in his death, he has also helped me. I wish I could turn back time and tell my brother to his face that I loved him and always have. I send that same message into the air and hope that he may grab it, wherever he might be.

It was also my brother's death that reiterated to me the importance of living life to the fullest but most of all living *your* life. That means making a conscious decision to change whatever it is that is preventing you from fulfilling what is important to you. I had to start living by that rule. My brother left Australia to live his life the way he wanted to and he found happiness. I know I can follow in his footsteps and find my happiness.

I do believe that things happen for a reason. I can't understand why my brother was taken, life is unpredictable, but I do know that I can learn from his life on this planet and use those lessons to improve my own life or way of thinking. The days I don't do that are wasted and life is too short to waste. I am sure if my late brother could speak he might agree with me.

CHAPTER 30

GRIEF IS A PERSONAL THING—DO IT YOUR WAY

> Grieving cannot be hurried
>
> (Unknown)

It was about eighteen months of living in the city with my friend that I started to find the arrangement was encroaching too much upon my need for personal space. This was an indication for me that my needs were changing and our friendship no longer met my needs. A sad reality but it happens to many friendships.

I felt unsettled and this caused me to think about our friendship and what it meant for me. I began to realise that I was repeating the mistakes of my previous relationships but this time with a person that I shared only a friendship with. I had found myself taking care of this person and then having an expectation that I would get what I gave in return. Again, I was seeking the same acceptance and approval I had always looked for. I allowed this friend to treat me in a manner that I did not deserve and again, I accepted that. I was living in a bubble in some way. I was so emotionally connected that at times it was smothering from both sides. I recognise too that I was in a comfort zone that I was not in a hurry to break out of.

We had created a space that we could both call our home. I needed a place where I could just relax and be myself. I believed I had found something close to it but that was to change when I began to grieve the loss of my friend to cancer. I needed to freely express my grief and loss at this time, and I felt my home was the place I could do it openly. I was well supported at work among my colleagues, but at home, I felt that I was getting different messages. I found myself beginning to feel lonely and isolated in my grief and taking on the negative messages that were coming my way. I can recall some of those messages like 'get over it', 'move on', 'she is the one that is dead and you being sad is disrespectful', 'you cried the other day now why the tears?'. These comments were very hurtful to me and lacked compassion at a very difficult time. Do they help you get over someone? Or just reinforce the fact that you are an emotional wreck. These comments discouraged me from speaking openly about my grief and therefore caused a greater feeling of isolation, loneliness and vulnerability.

I started to think that I was weak because I felt sad and that was coupled with a feeling of selfishness because I was the one who was still alive. In all honesty, I just wanted permission to express the loss I felt for such a beautiful person and that I was really going to miss her. My grief belonged to me and I wanted to grieve the way I thought was right for me. I was starting to realise that the environment I once called home was unhealthy for me. I accepted that my friend had good intentions and in his own way thought he was helping me but instead his comments were having a negative effect on me and that was not good for my emotional well-being.

Was I learning anything as I attempted to move forward step by step? Yes, I say I was but regardless of my lessons, I was still in a very vulnerable place and I could not allow my protective bubble to burst. However, I was reassured by my ability to sense that things were not quite the way I wanted them to be. I still did not make the connection that it was me allowing myself to be affected by the negative messages.

CHAPTER 31

SLOW STEPS IN A FORWARD DIRECTION— A SNAIL'S PACE

> In this world it is not what we take up but what we give up that makes us rich.
>
> (Henry Ward Beecher)

The years following my separation were emotionally chaotic and remained full of up and down moments even when my life appeared to be going well. The emotional roller coaster was relentless and just did not appear to have an end. You realise that you have little power over the ride ahead. You can't fight the gravitational pull and you are forced to surrender to it, time and time again.

On the emotional roller coaster, you are at the mercy of the steep inclines, dips, and curves, never knowing when the ride will end or how long it will last. For me, I never knew how long I would stay in the dips, which sharp turn would come next, or how hard the climb would be out of the steep dips. It was the unknown that made my journey forward so arduous and unpredictable.

I found life extremely challenging and unnerving after my separation. I didn't just have to contend with the roller coaster. I also had the relentless lapping wave of depression that would appear every now and then, just to keep me grounded and aware of how far I had already come. This was such an unpredictable time. The emotions stirred up during the many changes that a separation brings, made life hard for me and even harder for those people around me wanting to support me. I was still quite lost with no coordinates to even attempt to find some direction.

My friend Sue decided to take me away for the weekend just to give me a reprieve from my misery. As we headed off in the car, she played some music that reminded her of me.

The music was 'Breakaway' by Kelly Clarkson. I had not heard the song before, and when I listened to it I could understand why she thought of me. The words that resonated with me were dreaming of what could be and if I'll end up happy, I would pray. Trying hard to reach out but when I tried to speak out, felt like no one could hear me.

I'll spread my wings and I'll learn how to fly I'll do what it takes till I touch the sky. And I'll make a wish, take a chance, make a change, and breakaway.

Out of the darkness and into the sun, but I won't forget all the ones that I loved. I'll take a risk. Take a chance, make a change, and breaka . . . way.

I listened to these words and I felt they really captured how I was feeling at the time. Sue talked about why these words reminded her of me. I had spoken to her some years earlier about wanting to leave my marriage, and when I did eventually leave, she saw me as finally breaking away. The lyrics for me meant that I had to do whatever it took to find my happiness, and even though there was going to be a lot of dark times, I would eventually move into the sun. Most importantly along the way I would not forget the love I felt for my children and the people around me. I felt that I took a chance making that change in my life, and although I felt like I had no direction at times, I at least had some hope. These words gave me that hope at a time I felt hopeless.

I purchased the album and the songs became representative of my journey and struggle during the difficult times. When I was feeling anxious and distressed or unable to cope, I would play it. I played it sometimes three or four times over at a time depending on how my emotions were swinging. If I woke in the middle of the night unable to sleep, I played the album. I found the music was so calming and reassuring for me, it often helped me to get back to sleep. Music has always lifted my spirits and soothed my soul. This song and many of the other songs on the album helped me through my emotional pain. It is important that you find your own music that can soothe your soul through your pain. The words gave me faith that the hard times ahead of me were going to be worth the pain.

My work as a police officer was probably the most stable part of my life at that time. After leaving my children with their father, I chose to live with other people in shared arrangements. I did not have a lot of other options due to my financial position, but in particular, I did not want to be alone. I had not lived on my own at any time in my life, so I chose to bubble wrap myself in the safe surroundings of a few good friends. I had felt so insecure in my home life previously that I just wanted a few people to be by my side and create a little bit of stability for me.

One of my friends at the time was someone I had met through my work. I was drawn to him instantly because of his charisma and natural ability to make anyone feel important or special. He was funny and had a playful sense about him. As a colleague, he guided me professionally in an area that was new to me but at the same time allowed me to spread my wings and allow my life experience to flow freely. He kept a watchful eye on me as I found my feet, and it was not long before we had an inseparable connection to each other.

I found him to be magnetic in nature where no matter what I was doing at the time, I was drawn to him. I wanted to experience the world in that playful sense that he often communicated because I could see a resemblance of myself in him. He gave freely of his hugs and this was perfect for me. He was a good friend and protected me at a time that my vulnerabilities were exposed like a bare neck to a vampire. We became like family and shared open communication. This was a breath of fresh air because I had not experienced that previously. I felt like I could talk to him about anything and never feel threatened by rejection, judgement, or ridicule.

We shared a strong emotional relationship, which for me at the time was refreshing and exhilarating. I had not had that same emotional connection for such a long time and I realised how important this type of relationship was for me. I embraced his friendship whole heartedly and committed myself to him, baring both my emotions and generosity of friendship. His family also extended themselves to me and I became part of something that I treasured. Everything about him ignited a flame in me that had been extinguished for a long time. I did not know I could feel so alive in the midst of such turmoil. My passion for life was returning. I had found a secure platonic friendship that I would treasure.

A stable home was important to me, and because we shared a kindred spirit, I thought living with him would be perfect. We got on very well and I loved his company. We supported each other and lived a relatively simple existence. I shared some wonderful times with him and his family. It was a part of my life that has given me some wonderful memories.

It was around that time that I travelled overseas to Los Angeles for a second time. I was accompanied by another male friend. On our last night in Los Angeles we went out for a few drinks. After a few hours I became tired, so I walked the short distance back to our shared hotel room.

An hour or two later, I was snuggled up in bed in our hotel room when I heard two voices; one was my friends and the other was unknown to me. My friend introduced me to his new companion whilst they grabbed a drink from the minibar and then left the room. I was still awake when I heard them both return. I lay quietly in bed when I started to hear some heavy breathing happening in the bed next to me. I presumed that my presence would be respected and not devalued in the manner that it was about to be.

Well, this was not going to be the case when things intensified. I did not know what to do. Here I was in my mid forties feeling like a helpless child thousands of miles from home. Instead of sitting up and telling them to go elsewhere, I felt so inept in myself and went into an anxious frenzy of disbelief. Here I was again reluctant to cause conflict or confrontation even though I knew that I had the right to protest.

I lay there for a while, trying to find some answer to the question of what I should do. I felt frozen. I was seeing the bubble that I was living in back home in Australia burst. I took this incident really hard and it was a huge wake-up call for me and reflected the path I had taken since my separation. Whilst I was trying to figure out why I continued to be so vulnerable and lacking assertiveness they moved into the bathroom.

In my state of disbelief, I got dressed and left the room. At 2.45 a.m. I found myself walking the dark and lonely streets of Los Angeles. I walked twenty minutes to the all-night diner and sat pouring tears into their serviettes. I knew at that point, my path in life had to change and I needed to step out of the bubble. I realised that when you allow someone to treat you with disrespect then you begin to lose respect for yourself. I was on my own in life and I realised it was time for me to stand up and be strong or my life would continue the same way.

I sat in the diner until about 4.30 a.m. then started to walk back to the hotel. The streets of Los Angeles were empty and I felt nervous when a male pulled over in his car and started to slowly come up beside me. I was freaking out because my police officer background told me that I should never have put myself in such a situation. I was a mother of two, walking the streets of Los Angeles by myself, and it was stupid of me. I had chosen this option instead of standing up and voicing my disapproval. The strangest thing about that moment was that my thoughts were not on this incident but on the fact that my bubble had burst and it was time to face my life as an independent woman. This notion was frightening for me and something that I had been avoiding. I thank my lucky stars that I did not succumb to foul play in the early morning of that night whilst I was alone on the streets of Los Angeles. I learnt a clear lesson this night that it was my responsibility to look after myself, and if I didn't, then no one else would do it for me.

I learnt so much about myself that night in Los Angeles. I learnt that I was letting people treat me in a manner that I didn't deserve. I learnt that I had an expectation that others would look out for me and that expectation was unrealistic. I had entered into just a friendship and subconsciously begun to repeat the same old mistakes again, the same mistakes I had previously made in my marriage and in the relationship with my parents and all those men that I had encounters with during my adolescent years. Had I not learnt anything? Or was it that I was not willing to step outside of my comfort zone and take a risk by standing up for myself?

I had stayed in my comfort zone by creating a bubble, where I could freeze time and avoid responsibility. It was getting to the point where I needed my mistakes to hit me like a brick being thrown at my head and wake myself up to what I was doing.

I returned to Sydney knowing this information but feeling incapable of changing my circumstances. I think I believed I had too much at stake and that being treated in that manner was better than going it alone, but it was time for me to stand up and be counted. That night forced me into action where I was ready to stand up for myself.

A few months passed and I made the decision to change my living arrangements as well. I had grown so much of recent times and I felt ready to take the next step. The friendship with my flatmate had run its course like most friendships. I was starting to unwrap a very significant layer of self-doubt about going out on my own. I doubted my ability to survive on my own, and I was scared but it was something I needed to do.

I decided it was time to move out of my shared living arrangement. I decided to take on the unit by myself for a period of two months until it could be rented to someone else. This was a period of time over the Christmas break and the first time I had lived alone since I separated.

CHAPTER 32

A CHRISTMAS TO FORGET—SO MANY MEMORIES

> No matter how far we travel, the memories will follow in the baggage car.
>
> (August Strindberg)

I decorated the unit in Christmas cheer with the same passion that I had always done. I loved Christmas time and this year I was lucky to have the day off. My children were coming over on Christmas Eve and we were going to have a nice dinner and then a slow relaxing breakfast on Christmas day. I planned to return them to their father around lunchtime. This year I would be spending Christmas alone so seeing my children was really important to me.

We spent a wonderful evening together but my plans for Christmas day changed when I realised they needed to be home around 10 a.m. When I heard this, I took a gulp and then agreed so not to make things difficult for my children. Let's face it; I felt that I had made their life difficult enough. I blamed myself for many things and felt guilty about the rest. I was unforgiving of myself and felt so much like a failure. It wasn't funny.

We had a lovely breakfast, and I enjoyed the time I had with them, but it was time I drove them home to their father. When we arrived at the address, I drove my car along the long driveway and parked just next to the carport, close to the front door.

In the back of my mind was the thought that I was going home to an empty house and in the back of my throat was that lump I was becoming so familiar with. It was all part of the difficulties of divorce, and sometimes I just knew that I had to accept the not so great stuff like home alone for Christmas in return for a path to eventual happiness. I remember a voice inside me saying 'you are going to be OK, just knock on the door, wish them a Merry Christmas and get out of here'

I walked up to the front door with the persona that everything was OK. It was Christmas and I wanted to be seen by my children as merry. I was struck by the vision of a wreath hanging in pride of place on the front door. The wreath was familiar to me because I had purchased it many years ago and frilled it up with a big bow and some extra Christmas berries. Each year of the past twelve or so married years, I had placed the wreath on the front door of our family home. I looked at the wreath and felt a hit of adrenaline take over my body. My palms started to sweat and my hands began to shake. I could feel my heart pounding in my chest and my breathing become fast and shallow. My eyes focused on the wreath when the door opened and I got a glance of my ex husband and his new partner waiting to accept the arrival of the children. *But these were my children who were about to disappear behind the door that holds the wreath I hung on our family home for the past twelve or so years.* I gulped a bucket of air as I made an attempt to smile and say Merry Christmas. The words seemed meaningless as I felt my emotions start to swirl around me in an attempt to send a flood of tears excreting from my eyes. I sucked in another gulp of air in an attempt to compose myself, long enough to kiss my children goodbye. I wished them well and made a run for the car trying to make it look like I was calmly going about my business.

I saw that there were a few short strides towards my car, and as I took each stride, I felt my legs turning to jelly. I got into my car, sinking into the driver's seat while the gulps of air turned into gasps for breath as I felt the emotions flood my body like a mass of water rushing into a small container.

I felt overwhelmed with grief and loss for a life I once had. I had just left my children at a home displaying a sentimental wreath that had so much meaning for me for such a big part of my life. The children were behind the door where I was meant to be for the rest of my life. My children were in another family now, and just to add to my distress, I pictured them smiling and laughing whilst sitting around the table. I was sitting outside in my car on my own, ready to drive home to an empty unit and spend Christmas day by myself. To make things worse, the trip was only going to take twenty minutes.

I recalled then a quote that I had seen on a demolition truck that said something like 'all we leave are the memories'. I was devastated. Christmas day was a day that had made so many special memories for me. I felt like the rubbish being taken away by the demolition truck. My emotions were spiralling and the grief hit me smack, bang in the face that Christmas day. I did not want to celebrate anything I wanted to drown myself in my sorrows. I made it to the mid afternoon without hearing from anyone that day. I felt so alone. The wreath had caused my heart to shatter into a million pieces, and I could not detract my thoughts from that vision and what it represented to me.

I attempted to drown my sorrows in a bottle of wine, had toast for my Christmas dinner, and washed it down with a sleeping tablet. I wanted the day to end and I wanted to be numb and I wanted the tears to stop. I turned off my phone so I could not hear the silence anymore. I drifted off to sleep and would occasionally wake-up long enough for the emotional flood gates to reopen and then I would cry myself back to sleep.

Thank God, the sun rose for another day as my alarm went off in the morning, and I had to go to work. I was so glad I had work that day and I felt like work needed me more than anyone else and I was so thankful for that. I looked at myself in the mirror that morning and said, 'I am so glad that day is over and today is a new one'. This new day was boxing day and I was going to be protecting the people of Sydney whilst they shopped till they dropped at the well advertised sales.

Does that beat staying at home crying some more?
A B S O L UT E LY it does.

CHAPTER 33

THE IRONY OF THE JOB—ANOTHER SHARED MOMENT

> Often, we are too slow to recognize how much and in what ways we can assist each other through sharing such expertise and knowledge.
>
> (Owen Arthur)

I brushed myself off and put on my blue uniform making sure that I looked smart and professional. I dabbed some cream on my puffy swollen eyes and patted them with cool water. I donned my hat and my appointments belt, loaded my firearm and holstered it. I was in business for the day protecting the community. The memories of a miserable, horrible Christmas day were gone but never to be forgotten.

I teamed up with another female and we stood close to the doors of the major department store.

We both looked very professional and immaculate in our police uniform. I asked her, 'How was your Christmas?'

Her eyes started to glimmer as the tears began to flow and she told me of her sad Christmas, after the tragic loss of someone very special in her life only a few short months before. She went on to tell me how difficult it was for her to share her grief with the rest of the family because they were unable to cope. This added to her grief because she could not communicate her sadness to anyone and that left her feeling alone and isolated.

I gave her some words of support and then I relayed my story. We laughed at the irony of it all. Here we are two women in blue, looking immaculate protecting the community, while we hold back the tears of a nightmare Christmas day. Our stories were so different but we could relate to the grief and feelings of isolation. We looked the part that day, we were professionals and we both found solace in our work. We shared so much of ourselves that day to each other, and we both left feeling not so alone in our sadness.

When I returned to the police station at the end of my shift, the heaviness of my emotional few days hung over me. I got into the lift and my sergeant was standing there. This was the same sergeant that I supported that night in the bar when he told me how much he missed his children and the same sergeant that had taken his children on their holiday.

He said, 'Hey luv, how was your Christmas?' I welled up in tears and told him a brief version of the wreath on the door.

He said, 'I know luv, it's hard, I've been there'.

I said, 'And you know serg? The funniest thing is that it was the ugliest wreath you have ever seen' and with that we both laughed.

I took comfort from this sergeant because I knew that he could relate to my pain and it did not take more than a few words for him to understand what I was trying to say. His words healed a little bit of my pain that day and as he placed his hand on my shoulder in support I felt not so alone and that someone cared.

CHAPTER 34

THE ILLUSION OF FAMILY—MY ANGEL LANDLORD

> Consider whether a particular problem or pattern keeps repeating itself in your life. If it does, this is the voice of your Inner Self, calling you again and again to wake up.
>
> (Juan Nakamori)

It was not long until I was ready to move out of the unit.

I had so many good memories in that place, but I knew in my heart it was the right time to leave. I went from the unit to a spare room at my sister's place. This was a temporary arrangement, but I was looking forward most of all to spend some time with my sister and her partner. They were located close to the famous Coca-Cola sign at Kings Cross and this meant it was easy for me to get to work with a short walk through Hyde Park, Sydney.

I settled in and it appeared to me to be working well. I was working in the station during that time as part of the education team for the police officers and in particular, the new probationary constables. My background was training and I enjoyed assisting my colleagues in their academic and operational roles.

It was at this time that my personal life started to impinge on my ability to work freely within the workplace. I felt some tension crossing into my work environment which could not be avoided easily. I saw this as an opportunity to make a change. I spoke to my superior about my concerns and I was reassured by the fact that he was very concerned and supportive but in any case I requested at that time, to be considered for a transfer. I did not want to have my professional standing questioned or left open to ridicule particularly after I had worked so hard to protect it.

I was able to secure a transfer within days. I felt torn about leaving the workplace that supported me so well but I knew I needed to start fresh.

Within a few days I was on leave and when I returned to work I was starting at a new station out in the western suburbs of Sydney. I had requested that station because I was familiar with the west and it was a very busy station. I liked to be busy because work was everything to me at that time.

I settled in very well and from the first day in the station I was happy and felt really welcomed. I was put into a team that was very supportive and hard working. I became one of the team, part of the family and no one knew anything about me and that is the way it was going to stay. I trusted my colleagues completely from a professional standing, but I was not going to let them know too much about myself because of my past experience. I had learnt some very good lessons about trust, loyalty, and friendship.

I remained at my sister's place even though the travel was now consuming a lot of my time.

Things appeared to be going well at my sister's place. I was enjoying having my sister back in my life and I felt a sense of security.

I'd had my fair share of rejection in my life leading up to the time I stayed with my sister so I became settled feeling that I was in the safe realms of my family. My stay became lengthened to around four months whilst I was attempting to rebuild my savings and move into a rented place. I was fearful that I could not make it on my own due to my financial constraints and this led me to procrastinate in my decision-making. I was well and truly in my comfort zone.

Everything changed one night and I found myself having to make the decision to move. I was beginning to think that the roller coaster was parked behind me just waiting to swoop when I started to get too comfortable.

Yes! I was back in tears but I felt I had no time to waste so I got onto the internet and typed in shared accommodation. I got a list of home shares, house sitting, and various other alternatives.

I was distressed yet again, but I was getting used to that and therefore I just kept wiping the tears from my face before they short circuited my laptop. It was now midnight and I saw a granny flat advertised. I put my name out there and my interest. It was about five minutes later that I got a reply to my request for information.

The landlord said, 'What area are you looking at?'

I said, 'I work in western Sydney'.

The landlord said, 'Would the hills district suit you?'

I said, 'Yes'.

This conversation happened over a period of three hours and ended with an exchange of phone numbers at around 2 a.m. The alarm went off at 4.30 a.m., and in my sorry state, I put on my uniform and headed to work. I drove down the M4 freeway crying and sobbing trying to compose myself before arriving at work. I attended to my face in the change room before I stood with my colleagues at the morning meeting. I looked the part as usual in my blue uniform.

The first job we attended was a house fire, fairly routine with all the occupants accounted for. The next job was a deceased person. He had not got up for breakfast and when the family went to wake him, they realised that he had died during his sleep. The family were understandably upset as you would expect, and I supported them in my professional manner as I always did. We were at the location for several hours and in the middle of the day, I returned to our vehicle to make a phone call to the landlord of the granny flat. We agreed to meet that evening at the location.

At the end of my work day, I went straight to the banks automatic teller machine and drew out enough money for a partial deposit. On arrival at the house, I was met by the landlord. I was taken by her kindness straight away and I felt such a sense of relief that I had found a haven. She showed me such compassion and empathy within the first thirty minutes that I knew she had an insight into my emotional turmoil. She too had found hard times in her life and she knew what it was that I needed even before I did.

She said to me, 'You need some peace and looking after.'

She was my angel in the night that answered my distress call for accommodation over the internet, and when I met her, she was most definitely an angel. We did a deal that night, she accepted my deposit, and I could move in three days later.

CHAPTER 35

ALWAYS ROOM FOR FAMILY—YOU JUST HAVE TO MAKE IT!

> Families are the compass that guides us. They are the inspiration to reach great heights, and our comfort when we occasionally falter.
>
> (Brad Henry)

On the day that I moved in, I had a very good feeling about this little granny flat. As I walked in the front door, to the right was a lovely new bathroom that was mostly white with black feature tiles that depicted elephants. In front of me was a bedroom which had a queen-size bed and a wardrobe. The main room was about three metres by three metres and this was the living space with a small kitchenette and washing machine. The flat was completely self-contained so I needed very little of anything. The nicest thing for me was the peacefulness of the surrounds and the large window facing the lush garden and positioned to receive the morning sun.

My angel landlord greeted me with the house key and gave me the option of joining her and her other house guests at anytime I desired. I was in heaven with an angel living next door. I was close to work, which was perfect and finally on my own with benefits of company only just up the garden path. It took me only a few days to settle, but I knew that this was going to be a long journey to recovery and I was in the right place. I was broken and in deep grief over the direction my life had taken. I felt I finally belonged somewhere.

I was ready to face the future, and it was time to rebuild my life. I was supported in presence of the people around me but now it was time to support myself in planning of my future. I felt that my life was a mess and I now had the breathing space to get it on track. There was no one to influence me, no one to nurture, and no one to be waiting for me when I got home. Just me and that was a wonderful feeling. I was empty inside and felt drained of all my energy. I had very little left to give to anyone let alone myself but in amongst that feeling I had a sense of peace that this was part of the completion of my roller coaster.

It was in the granny flat that I started writing. I needed to get my feelings out somehow and the best place to put my feelings into words was on paper. I knew that my writing would heal some part of me along the way and I also wanted to be able to reflect on my journey at a later time.

I felt isolated from everyone at that time and I made the choice to keep my personal struggles to myself. I knew that I could only trust myself and that gave me some control. I was working hard as usual and long days. On my days off, I usually just chilled at home because I felt exhausted and had little energy for much else. I had very little money and started to fill my days by drinking heavily. This numbed the emotional pain to some degree. I found some cheap wine that cost very little and I started to drink on a daily basis. I knew my limits because of my job and my responsibility, so I chose not to drink on the days I was working.

Around the second week that I had moved into the flat, I was visited by my daughter and son. I was anxious about their visit because I did not want them to see me living in this little space. I knew they would worry about me, but at the same time, I knew in myself that this was the best place for me at the time. My daughter and son arrived and looked around. My daughter went straight to the fridge, opened the door, and glanced inside. She did the same to the pantry door and again glanced in there.

I said, 'Are you hungry?' 'What are you looking for?'

She replied, 'I am just checking you have enough food'

My son was just checking out the size of the television which was about 30 cm by 30 cm screen.

A few weeks went by when I was sitting at home and I thought to myself that it was time to have a glass of wine. I looked at the clock and it was only eleven o'clock in the morning. I knew then, that I was in trouble and was heading for an addiction to a substance that I grew up knowing the ramifications of that addiction. I made a conscious decision to monitor my drinking to the point of eventually stopping. I needed to take control of my life not destroy it. I also knew that the alcohol only numbs the pain momentarily, so this would hinder my ability to remain resilient. I needed resilience to push through the hard times ahead.

It was the innocence of my daughter's concern that played on my mind and I knew that she was genuinely worried about me. It was the little subtleties of life that kept me moving forward.

I had been in the granny flat for about seven weeks when I received a request from my ex husband to have my son overnight for two nights per week. I was aware that my son was having difficulties at home with the arrangement but I did not know to what extent.

I believe that my children were trying to protect me from what was really happening in their lives. I recognize that the situation for all of us involved was difficult. My daughter was older and able to remove herself to lesson any disruption in her life, but my son was stuck because of his age. I remember when I was a young adult feeling stuck and unable to escape my own home environment. For me, it did not mean that I loved my parents any less but I just needed to be where I wanted to be.

I was living on top of myself in this small self-contained granny flat, I felt I had little money to support myself let alone my son, and I was emotionally exhausted and in need of some respite. I worked shift work and there was no means of my son getting himself to school and there was still the problem of 'where was I going to put him two nights per week?'

All these thoughts were going through my head but were soon eliminated when I spoke to my son and I realised he had an anger inside him that I had not seen before. I sensed that it was his unhappiness that was the root of his frustration. I knew then that he needed me back in his life and although I could not give him a fulltime arrangement, I could hopefully satisfy some of his needs with quality time, two nights per week. I was after all his mother and it was time I stood up to that responsibility, whatever it took.

I spoke to my angel landlord and she felt that it was a perfect arrangement although I would be required to pay her some extra money. I was relieved by her kindness and compassion.

I jumped into action. I bought a blow-up mattress, bedclothes, and pillow to accommodate him.

Every night that he stayed, we would move all the furniture to one side and lay his mattress down in front of the fridge. Every morning we did the opposite to allow ourselves enough room to get some breakfast and prepare his lunch.

I purchased a laptop for his use so that he could attend to his homework. The food bill was extra and now I also had extra costs with petrol whilst driving him to and from school each day. Regardless of the extra strain on my budget, I soon realised that having quality time with my son was priceless and worth more than money.

The two nights we spent together were magical and I realised that my son wanted and needed me back in his life. We got on so well in our tiny space and he did not complain about anything.

The hardest thing for me was dropping him back home after our two days together. I could see the stress and anxiety begin to build as we got closer to his home. My son showed me that a sense of belonging was more important than your surroundings. He had the best of everything in his home environment, but he seemed happy for the two days that he stayed in my small granny flat. This lesson changed how I perceived my life. I realised that I could be much worse off and that I needed to change my way of thinking because I had my son's well-being to think about. I felt hope for the future and a new focus away from my own misery. I could see a glimmer of hope that I would survive this turmoil. Sometimes we need a knock on the head to be reminded what is important to us. It was time for me to get a knock on the head and I thank my ex husband for giving it to me.

CHAPTER 36

THE STRESS OF THE JOB—LIFE IS FRAGILE

> In any moment of decision the best thing that you can do is the right thing, the next best thing is the wrong thing, and the worst thing is nothing.
>
> Theodore Roosevelt

Around the same time I moved into the granny flat, I was trying to maintain a professional appearance at work amongst my team and colleagues. My new station was very family orientated because of the location and ages of my colleagues. This was different to my other station which had a higher percentage of young singles.

I felt part of the furniture very quickly and began to love my new station, thanks to my wonderful team.

One morning I started work at 9 a.m. On arrival, I was handed a missing person's case and instructed to make some enquiries. I read the initial report that was taken in the early hours of that morning.

I started to make extensive enquiries into their possible whereabouts. They had gone missing in what I thought were unusual circumstances. I traced their movements as best I could and whilst making my enquiries I began to build a picture in my head of the lives of the missing persons. I saw them as normal people trying to build a good life. Just a mother and daughter doing all the usual things that I would have been doing with my daughter when she was the same age.

A mother caring for the daily needs of her child was not out of the norm. A child attending school, playing with friends, and cuddling a favourite toy at night was characteristic of every child. These were two human beings going about their daily lives.

I spoke to anyone who had contact with the child, her friends, her peers, her school, and her neighbours. I stood in their rooms and saw personal items that would be no different to what I had in my own home. I saw photos of their smiling faces sitting on the bookshelf.

I asked to see the favourite toy that the child would have sought comfort from on so many occasions as my own children were comforted. I looked at the soft toy alone, without the child who expressed so much love for it and found soothing comfort from its mere presence.

I had a picture in my mind of this normal family but things just did not add up and it was not long before my gut feeling entered the equation.

After making numerous enquiries during the day, I handed the investigation over to the detectives. At the time I gave a verbal handover, I had grave fears for the safety of the two missing persons.

It was about one month later that their bodies were found and our worst fears were confirmed. I remember the afternoon well.

I started work late afternoon and as I entered the rear door of the station, I was told by my team sergeant that one body had been located and a team were searching for the other. They were believed to be the bodies of the two missing persons.

When I heard this news, I burst into tears and felt so sad for the victims and their family. In one sense I was relieved the family's wait for news was over and in another sense it was news I just did not want to hear. Nevertheless, the news hit me hard because I had such an involvement in the early part of the investigation.

I was just a police officer with only five-years experience when I realised that I had been standing in the same room as the murderer. He had no distinguishing features, he was just a man who neither stood out in the crowd nor was remarkable in anyway. I had put faces to names of the missing persons and they would be with me until today and I am sure for many years to come. A senseless tragedy like this you never forget.

I realised then that life was just so precious.

It was not long before the victim's husband was charged with two counts of murder. He would eventually be convicted and sentenced to the rest of his life in jail.

The family were also sentenced but to a life of grief and disbelief that their loved ones had met such a terrible end.

My colleague and I attended the memorial service in our own time. It was a mark of respect to the two victims and a message to the family that we cared for them at this terrible time. It was important for me to show the family that I cared.

I was overwhelmed with emotion on the day of the memorial service. I just could not fathom how someone could take the life of another and in particular an innocent child. My only pacifier was that they were together, just as they had been at birth.

This case was not over for me yet, next came the need for me to sit and write a detailed account of my enquiries in the form of a police statement. I was living in the granny flat alone. This was the first time I had been alone in my whole life. I had been surrounded by either family or friends in the past but this time I was solo.

I tried to tell some of my friends about the murder but they did not want to hear any details, so the conversation was changed pretty swiftly. I understood where they were coming from. It is confronting for anyone. We all hear about these things on the news and pretend we are immune to something like that happening. We listen to the details with interest and curiosity but we detach ourselves from the story as if it is a hollywood movie. That way we do not need to be concerned because we all think that something like that can't happen to us. I knew as a police officer it can happen.

I wanted to share with others my despair and feeling that life as we know it is not so great when things like this can happen. 'Is it any wonder that our emergency workers socialise together and commonly marry within the ranks?'

I felt so alone and isolated at this time and my best friend became the two for one white wine deal at the local bottle shop. It could not talk back to me but gave me a warm fuzzy feeling like someone cared.

I completed my statement and I found that I could not get this murder out of my head. I spoke to some of my work colleagues and they were visibly upset also. We helped each other and eventually I sought help from the employee's assistance program.

I did not feel this helped me personally because I don't believe anyone can have an understanding of the type of things police and emergency workers deal with every day. Yeah, sure, psychologists, counsellors, and psychiatrists know how the brain works and we definitely benefit from their expertise in times of trauma. I don't believe they can possibly have the same insight unless they have done the job themselves.

Thirty three years ago, I nursed a small child that died as a result of an accident. The only thing that I remember when I recall that moment is a vision in my mind of two lifeless little legs poking out of a nappy whilst lying listless on the huge bed. It took me a long time to stop thinking about the child's mother. On mother's day, every year, for at least ten years, I thought about how hard it must be for her.

I know that I will take that vision to my grave and I also know that I am not unique in thinking that. So many of my colleagues will be doing the same with their own visions. The debriefing that I received after the death of the small child in the emergency department was invaluable to my recovery, and although I can still recall that vision, I am not emotionally charged by it anymore.

The distinct difference for me between nursing and policing is that life is fragile and therefore people die, we all die, some prematurely, some as the result of a long illness, some as a result of an accident or at their own hands. The latter, policing deals with those same scenarios but additional to that is the fact that people die at the hands of another.

I decided after my involvement in the missing person's investigation it was an opportunity to learn a valuable lesson. That lesson was that my family and myself had to be my number one priority.

I had to learn something from this tragedy so that the deaths of this mother and child would not be in vain. It was the personal lessons for me that changed my perspective on my own life and how I lived it.

My children became my focus and my youngest in particular. I felt that no hurdle in my life was going to be as difficult as what these two missing persons endured and the grief and loss that their family members were suffering.

For me, I had to make a firm decision about my future and my priorities. My son needed me and wanted to be with me on a permanent basis and I knew that I had to make that happen. I did not believe I could rebuild my life whilst I remained in the police service. My wages as a registered nurse were significantly more than a police officer. I was burnt out because I had thrown myself into my work as an avoidance of my chaotic personal life and if I was to be out of nursing for any longer, I would have had to do a refresher course at my own expense.

The last and most important consideration for me was my psychological welfare. As a nurse I dealt with tragedy constantly, particularly within an emergency environment, but that was life. Life is fragile and death is inevitable for all of us. The difficult realisation for me was that other people could do such terrible things to another person. In a state of anger, revenge, drunkenness, or stupidity, it did not matter to me. No one deserves to have their life shortened because of another person's actions.

How do we find understanding and acceptance of these events and why should we?

The tragedy of the missing person's case happened at a time when I was ready to stand up and listen to the messages the incident was showing me in my personal life but it had taken its toll.

I needed time out and I was very fortunate to have a boss who understood my needs and supported my application for leave without pay. I was not ready to make a decision to leave a job that I loved so much and had worked so hard to obtain.

I was fortunately granted twelve months leave without pay to clear my thoughts and make my decision. I missed the job in a lot of ways but I gained my life back and that was my new priority.

I recognised the potential for long term psychological damage when police are confronted with these types of tragedies on a daily basis. My years of experience as an emergency nurse backed up my reasoning.

I no longer wanted to deal with the criminal element of society or witness the effects that serious crimes had on their victims.

After five months in the granny flat, my son and I moved into a house close to the hospital I began nursing at. The day we moved in together was the beginning of my true healing and the start of a promising future.

I was fortunate to be able to take one year off before making my decision to leave the job that had given me so much satisfaction. I lived my dream; I loved the job and the life lessons that being a police officer taught me. I eventually resigned from the police service but not without hesitation.

The day I handed in my badge and uniform brought such mixed emotion. I drove to the police station and parked my car in the local car park. I was shaking, anxious, and teary when I phoned one of my policing friends (Kristy). I needed reassurance that I was doing the right thing for me. She reminded me of the reasons I got to this point. I knew it was the right thing in my mind but I felt that policing was in my blood running through my veins and I wondered how I was going to live life without it. 'Would I find the same fulfilment in anything else that I would do?'. I had a passion for the job that is hard to explain. It grabs you wholeheartedly and overtakes you in an exhilarating way but at the same time it consumes you in a burdening way. The intensity of the role is not for the faint-hearted because we bare our soul to it. Too many times the individual police officer's soul is exposed.

It is like a roof exposed to the winter snow. The snow falls gradually over a period of time and as it falls the layer becomes thicker. While it keeps snowing the load becomes heavier and the weight of the snow starts to burden the structure holding the roof in position. Eventually the structure gives way and the roof caves in under the burden of weight.

The engineers think that they have built the roof to withstand the weight but have underestimated the burden that the snow can place on the structure. They had predicted the possible weight of snow falls from the average weather patterns over centuries but failed to account for extremes.

Policing can't prepare its officers for the weight of the burdens inflicted on their souls because the tragedies and criminal element in society never cease to shock us. Just when we hear what we think is the worst, we hear something even more so. Where there is a human element to trauma and tragedy, I don't believe we can understand how it can affect the individual souls of our police.

For me, I realised this about myself. I did not know what lay behind the doors of the next radio call. 'What was it that I was going to be dealing with next?' but this unpredictability was no different to my emergency nursing work. The difference for me was that I did not have faith that the NSW Police had the systems in place to protect my soul from collapsing under the weight. My policing colleague agreed and this confirmed to me that I was doing the right thing for me and therefore I handed in my badge and uniform. It was an emotional day and the end of a special part of my life. I have no regrets and will keep the fond memories of the job for the rest of my living days.

CHAPTER 37

THE IMPORTANCE OF PREVENTION— A SUPPORTIVE ENVIRONMENT

> Survivors are people who, in times of crisis or challenge, are able to: surmount their troubles by dint of their own efforts: discover strengths and abilities they didn't previously possess: gain something of lasting value from their experiences.
>
> (The Survivor Personality by Patti Westcott)

I look back on my nursing career spanning thirty plus years with great memories. It was not until returning to nursing after resigning from the police that I was reassured that I had done the right thing.

In the areas of nursing that I have worked, I have seen great human tragedy. I can't recall a time when I was not able to talk to a colleague about the hard days. Sometimes words did not need to be spoken but in their place was that facial expression that says 'I hear you'.

I had no doubt that I was in the right profession whilst nursing because it is a nurturing profession and I am a nurturer. We look after our patients with compassion and care. We look after each other with the same.

I experienced a version of the same in the police service and I have used the term camaraderie in an attempt to make a comparison. I saw some horrific sights whilst I was a police officer and heard some tragic stories. I consoled the victims, families, and bystanders that I had contact with during my normal work day.

I can also look back on a wonderful five-year career as a police officer with fond memories. At the same time I have to say that for me, I did not believe that I could get the same psychological support that I have come to assume from the nursing profession. This was the major consideration for me personally when I made the decision to resign.

It was not until after I had resigned that I became reassured that I had made a wise decision but one of my dearest friends (police officer) had not been so lucky.

I spoke to her on the phone recently and I was surprised to sense her feelings of guilt so I wrote her a letter in response. I wanted to express to her that someone understands her psychological trauma and that she should not listen to negative comments about her 'mortgage buster' (disability payout) when they have no idea of her suffering. It is only the close friends and loved ones that see the pain and suffering of our fallen comrades. Some don't even get to see that because their loved ones have chosen to take their own lives instead.

I believe when we place a nametag like 'mortgage buster' onto a disability payment then it changes the perception of that payment. The focus becomes on paying the mortgage instead of paying for the ongoing medical support that our injured police may require.

There is no doubt that wherever we live in the world there will always be people who will attempt to take what is not rightfully theirs or what they don't deserve. Call it fraud, rorting, or abuse of a system that was set up with some good intentions.

I believe that we must stop to think and remember that amongst the rorting are the legitimate, whose pain is exacerbated by our judgements. All too often our criticism is wrongly directed towards the recipient where it should be directed at the system itself.

The Sydney Morning Herald printed part of my letter under the heading Disability Scheme 'A fair go for hurt police—and for taxpayers, too' on the 24 November 2011. I had written it much earlier in response to that conversation I had with my former colleague and dear friend. I sent it in after I saw the protest march to Parliament House by uniformed police (my former colleagues) supported by their association. The full letter went like this.

> There have been two times in the past three years that I have looked in the 'changes in the force' section of the NSW police news magazine. This is the official journal of the police association of New South Wales.
>
> When I looked and saw two names so familiar to me, I felt a sense of sadness that a special journey was over. One of those names was mine and the other, a very special friend.
>
> We met in 2003 at the Goulburn police college as we commenced the training for our new career as a NSW police officer. At no time, could we foresee the future or know where our individual journeys would take us.
>
> On graduation day, our paths separated but our friendship continued. Our individual aspirations of long careers as NSW police officers were in amongst our hopes and dreams for our futures.
>
> For me, the fond memories of the career I loved will stay with me forever, but my decision to leave came without regret. I recognised early in my career that the psychological toll was going to be too high if I continued along my chosen path.

Sadly, everyday I worked, I became aware of the damaged souls around me and for many, the cost had been too high and they could no longer continue to serve their community. The essence of their true selves had been scarred by the destruction of life around them.

These traumatised people gave so much of themselves for a job that pays no dividends or offers any glory. The organisation's table still turns, while their wounded constabulary are struggling to survive the turmoil in their minds caused as a direct result of their service to humanity.

I saw my future as being one of those wounded, so I chose to leave before the often irreparable damage was done and I would join the many who continue to live in turmoil, well after they hand in their badge. My thoughts are with those many police officers who for varied reasons are no longer able to perform their duty within the organisation but who are suffering in isolation instead.

My friend is one of those wounded souls. My dearest friend offered her soul to the job and worked tirelessly with no expectation of reward but only asked that she would surface unscathed. This has not been the case and no amount of money can replace the dreams we both had for a future in a career, we worked so hard to be part of.

We hear so much about the payouts given to our troubled comrades and we have cleverly, but thoughtlessly labelled them 'mortgage busters'. In my experience as a registered nurse working in emergency for over twenty years, I have seen the emotionally damaged all too often. I can assure you that no amount of money can restore someone's soul when it has been broken and traumatised by the day to day exposure to tragedy that our police officers encounter.

My friend is a survivor and she deserves, every cent of money that is rewarded to her but no amount of money will bring back the same person that she *was on that day we graduated. However, there is always hope amongst the emotional pain that all we be OK.*

These people need our support and understanding for the rest of their lives. Ignorance to their emotional scars, denial of the longevity of the emotional scars, and deprivation of adequate recovery payouts will destroy the lives of our wounded.

On police remembrance day each year, let us not only remember the fallen, but also the long term wounded.

When I think about my friend and her trauma, I feel saddened and I ask myself, 'Would the same type of debriefing that I received so readily in nursing, have made a difference?' I believe the answer to be 'yes'.

I worked with a constable one day when he attended his first deceased. He was hesitant in dealing with the family because he had not been exposed to such open displays of emotional distress. He wanted to do his best at comforting them at this difficult time. I was in the fortunate position that I could use my experience to assist him. I commend him for recognising his lack of experience and asking for support.

He did a fantastic job under very difficult circumstances, but when we returned to the confines of our police vehicle, he was visibly shaken. On return to the station he said to the supervisor, 'I have just been to my first deceased, do I need to attend some debriefing?' The supervisor replied, 'Consider yourself debriefed'. I was disappointed by this comment but unfortunately not surprised.

I followed up on my colleague during his days off and made sure he was OK.

NEVER GOOD ENOUGH... UNTIL NOW

I know that the above does not reflect everyone in the police service but one is one too many. When I needed support one evening, I went to the senior officer and requested some time to talk. The response from my superior was 'If it is going to take longer than five minutes, then it will have to wait'. I went home via the bottle shop that night. These two incidences highlight the reasoning behind my resignation.

I began my nursing training only a few years after the Granville train disaster. Our nurse's training reiterated the lessons that came from that tragedy. Debriefing was one of those lessons.

I wonder some days if our emergency services organisations have forgotten those important lessons that stemmed from that terrible event.

I have come from two unique professions. One is male dominated and one is female dominated. It is a documented fact that men communicate differently to women. I have observed this in both my careers, my personal life and I see it in my children. In a macho environment, men are even less likely to communicate their feelings than that of a female-dominated environment.

I was in tears one day at the police station I was working at the time and I was told that, 'I don't think you are cut out for this job'. You can imagine my thoughts towards this person. I can't say exactly what I thought because of the language but I was disappointed at his ignorance. Imagine if I had been twenty years younger, I may well have believed him.

During my police training in Goulburn, I remember a session which touched on the tragedies of the job and the effect that it may have on attending police. The session presenter encouraged us to speak to someone about any concerns or if we found ourselves needing to talk to someone. It sounded good and very supportive, but I can't help think about the constable who attempted to speak out. If we read between the lines he most likely wanted to talk about his first deceased and took the opportunity to ask. The 'macho' response that he received relinquished the opportunity in one fowl swoop.

I believe that the NSW Police have systems in place in an attempt to identify and support those within their constabulary who attend to traumatic events or crisis. I personally did not have faith in the delegated individuals within the police service to abide by those systems and implement them.

Until systems are adhered to then the cost of disability payouts will always be on the agenda. The goal should be to reduce the numbers requiring payouts by attempting to prevent the injury occurring in the first place or promote early intervention.

It is much easier to stop the snow from building up before it gets to the point where the roof caves in.

CHAPTER 38

TUCKING MY CHILDHOOD INTO BED—FOR GOOD

> Life will keep bringing you the same test, over and over again, till we pass it
>
> (Unknown)

There is no getting around the fact that I have carried my childhood scars for far too long. I was severely traumatised by the day that I had to cower in the corner listening to my father abuse and beat my mother. I would not wish that on any small child. Sadly though, I know from my policing experience that there are children who are suffering at this very moment.

I don't want you to think that I have been thinking about my childhood every day of my waking hours because that is not true. What I have done is carried on the beliefs that I developed from those incidents.

The human brain is programmed to keep us alive. When our survival is threatened and we don't feel safe, we create strategies in our mind. We do this in an attempt to avoid whatever it is that is threatening us, therefore keeping us safe from further harm. It does not have to be a physical threat but can be triggered by a response to fear.

As a child, our strategies may not necessarily make sense but as an adult, we can still create them and have some insight into knowing when they are no longer of use to us. An example might be that one of your bosses is difficult to get along with. You clash and each time you have any contact with them, you feel humiliated or stupid. This has an impact on how you feel about yourself and your confidence deflates. You create a strategy to protect yourself from further harm and in this instance you choose avoidance. Your strategy to avoid this person may be to work different days, have your meal breaks when they are usually in the office, ring in sick the day your appraisal is due, or chuck in a job that you love just to get away. You make most of these decisions from a conscious level.

As a child in the same situation you may bring your boss lollies and invite him to your birthday party. You may do all your bosses chores for him, wear his favourite colour clothes, and share your favourite toys.

A child will do anything to try and gain acceptance but when this does not work they feel it is because of them, not because the boss needs a good kick up the proverbial. As an adult you change jobs and get a new boss who treats you appropriately. A child might think that every boss is the same and therefore will keep using that strategy well after its use by date whether they need to or not. The strategy gets stored in the subconscious and may cause problems for the child when he brings the boss lollies and everyone thinks he is after a promotion. All he is trying to do is prevent being made to feel stupid and humiliated as had happened in the past.

I believed that I needed to achieve great things in life because I was needing love, acceptance, and approval. When I did not get that, I just went on to something else that I perceived as a worthy achievement. I failed to stop and celebrate anything because if it did not come with acceptance from my mother, then it was not a good enough achievement. By this stage I was looking for the next.

I did not stop to think that my mother may not even be thinking anything like that and when I shared this with her recently, she said, 'Why would you want to do that?'. It was perfectly clear to me then that it was my own thinking that was screwing me up, not anyone else's.

'Why hadn't I seen that before? Are you sitting around waiting for someone to give you something that you are never going to get from them?' I was. It was like my mother and I were living on two different planets. I developed that strategy as a child but never checked in to see if it was really working for me as an adult. When this was pointed out to me in a life coaching session that I attended, I was able to put it to bed almost instantaneously. Since then I have been consciously making myself celebrate anything that I achieve because that is so much more positive. I felt lighter and liberated. Then I had the light bulb moment and thought 'Oh my god! What other strategies have I been relying on and to my dismay I could uncover numerous'. I had found my answer to my low self-esteem. I had been living at the effect of everything. These strategies in the form of beliefs were holding me in the past too scared to break away from them. Too scared to move into the unfamiliar and be the cause of my own reality. Yes, I could do this in my professional life but not in my personal life.

That is when it really hit me that the responsibility for my past was mine and mine alone. *But* 'You know what?' It was the first time in my life that I could move into a new phase where I would be completely responsible for what happens to me. I felt so liberated and free. After all this time I can now say that I am my own statue of liberty!

What happened in my childhood family home cannot be changed but it can be disempowered. In the past few years I have in a way conducted a post-mortem on the effect that day has had on me and I have been gobsmacked at what I uncovered. One intense traumatic incident coupled with an insecure home life has infiltrated every area of my life. I am so glad I discovered this at fifty instead of eighty. I would not want to waste one more day on old beliefs. It is time to start living. Now I know exactly what Dr Phil meant when he was talking about not wasting another day of your life.

If I could draw a comparison to how one incident could create and infiltrate so many of my beliefs I would have to say it was like my computer. I know little about computers and anyone close to me knows that my frustration level rises whenever I have a problem.

A computer glitch might start with a little message popping up on your screen caused by an accidental tap of a key that you have no idea what its function is. The message box pops up as a result of your stray finger.

It asks you a question you don't understand and the only way you can get it to go away is by choosing an option of yes or no. You have no idea, so you make a guess and hope for the best. The next thing you know you are bombarded with several message boxes that ask you again to answer yes or no. After several of these and many guesses later, you find that the whole workings of your computer have changed and you no longer have its co operation. Those of us not computer savvy expect that our computer should know what we want and just do it, without giving us grief. We see it as unreasonable for the computer to ask us a question we can't answer and we did not want in the first place.

We start to believe that the computer is against us. Then when we enlist someone's help, we find that we have answered the questions the wrong way. By this time the problem has infiltrated the workings of the computer and we're stuffed. It is then that you have to retrace your steps to resolve the problem. Initially everything goes back to normal and you get a reprieve from the message box. At a later date when you go into a file that you have not opened for some time another problem comes up. When this occurs several times over any given period you soon realise that these issues are all related to that first pop up box where you answered yes when you should have said no.

'Are you getting my point?' The glitch has lingered in the memory of your computer only to come back at a later date when you hit that same key again. You don't need the glitch, but you can only get rid of it if you know how! A belief is the same as a glitch. You have to seek out where it originated from before you can delete it. I bet that all you computer experts reading this are attempting to find a solution to the glitch as fast as you can without delving into the hard drive. That is our natural response and that is similar to when we hear move on, get over it, pump up, put the past behind you and of course there are people much worse off. The fact is that everyone's computer glitch is unique to them so too is the timing around it. It has taken me nearly forty years to get it. If it takes you ten then you are doing better than me. Then again some people never get it. 'Does it really matter?' It only matters if it matters to you!

I looked back on my childhood so many times during my life but for some reason it was through foggy glasses and I could not see any clarity around the lessons. It was not until I experienced the adversity of recent years that I finally got it, but it took time to download. I think that time was necessary so when I did get it I was ready to confront what I needed to.

Today, I can see reasoning and understand how my patterns of thinking and the beliefs attached to those patterns have impacted on my thoughts and decisions. When I realised this, I could see repetition in the way I was living my life. I was repeating my mistakes over and over again. This realisation was a major catalyst for change for me. I wanted to learn from my mistakes and not be a prisoner to them anymore.

I want to share with you some of my debilitating beliefs and I hope you might be able to reflect on some of yours. I believe we all have them to some degree.

I did not know as a child that I should have been the one that was protected. I was too young to understand adult stuff.

I formed the belief that I should have protected my mother and stopped my father from breaking her nose, *but* I was only about ten years of age and had no way of knowing what to do. I did not have the maturity or skills to figure it out. I felt guilty about my sister having to protect me as well. I felt that I should have tried to help her. It is time I forgave myself for that. I thought it was somehow my fault that my parents were arguing so I blamed myself.

I wanted the police officer to take me away from the house because I was so scared, but he did not. I felt abandoned by someone that I thought should have protected me but the law was different then.

My father did not talk to us for weeks after the argument. He stayed in his room and played his mouth organ. I felt rejected by that and felt undeserving of his attention because he would not talk to me.

I tried so hard to help my mother so that she would not get stressed and therefore they would not argue anymore. I tried to be 'miss goody two shoes'. I tried to be perfect.

I stopped speaking out about things that I wanted or felt important to me. I associated speaking out with conflict and confrontation. I lost the voice inside me so kept quiet and said nothing about anything that had the potential to cause conflict or confrontation.

I did not feel appreciated because my mother only seemed to notice what I didn't do, instead of appreciating what I did do to help her.

I became independent so she would not have to worry about me and therefore she would suffer less stress. My desire for independence drove me away from the family home and put a distance between the people I loved most.

I worked to lighten her financial burden as I could pay for my own things, but when she did not recognise my efforts, I just kept taking on more work.

I set out to achieve as much as I could to try and make her proud. When I did not get her approval I just kept going onto something else never stopping to celebrate any of my achievements before moving on to the next.

I wanted to fix everything for her and therefore went on to try and fix everything for everybody.

I put everyone's emotional needs before my own always expecting that I would be appreciated for it.

I expected people to treat me the way I would want to be treated myself, but I set no boundaries for myself and therefore let people walk all over me.

The list goes on and I find it interesting that I feel quite detached from the above. I have after all these years relinquished ownership of them because these beliefs don't serve a purpose anymore. I am an adult now and I no longer need these beliefs to survive in a dysfunctional family or the big wide world.

Once I recognised the messages and beliefs which have influenced me throughout my life, I soon realised that my thinking patterns were no longer serving me in a positive way. They were in fact decaying the true essence of who I am and want to be.

This recognition came with two very clear messages and not ones that I found easy to digest. Next came, the daunting prospect of having to take responsibility for everything that had happened in my life and with responsibility came the need to embrace forgiveness.

I thought to myself 'Well, I am strong and willing to accept that I had made choices in my life, none of us are perfect, and so this part should be easy'.

Well, that comment could not have been further from the truth. All of a sudden a whole bunch of words popped into my head and gave me one huge lump in my throat and very sweaty palms.

You may be able to resonate with some of the words, but I am sure that you would also have some of your own. My words are victim, blame, guilt, remorse, regret, shame, and resentment, anger, judgement, disrespect, rejection, and undeserving. Each one of these words highlighted to me different areas of my life; however, I don't believe they represented the type of person that I am today.

It is not easy to look back with hindsight and see that you have clung on to old beliefs, messages, or strategies. I have not lived my life consciously thinking about my childhood, but obviously the beliefs and strategies that I used to survive have stayed with me.

I spent my life searching for answers to the wrong question. I was asking, 'How could I heal the pain from my childhood?' When in reality I should have been asking, 'How can I change the beliefs I created during my childhood?' I was not consciously aware that I was living my life by defunct beliefs. Once I understood that, it was like a ten tonne weight was lifted from my shoulders and the fog was lifted from my eyes. My sight was now crystal clear and I can finally say it is time for me to 'move on'.

CHAPTER 39

A LETTER TO MY MOTHER—I HAVE ALWAYS LOVED YOU

> I was never one to patiently pick up broken fragments and glue them together again and tell myself that the mended whole was as good as new. What is broken is broken—and I'd rather remember it as it was at its best, than mend it and see the broken places as long as I lived.
>
> (Margaret Mitchell)

I am so sorry that you had such a violent and abusive childhood. It must have been awful.

You too were just a child in need of protection and love and you did not get that. You lost your innocence at the hands of your own parents. You did not deserve to be treated in that manner.

I am sorry that you endured something similar from my father. No one deserves to be abused either physically, verbally, emotionally, financially, or sexually.

I want you to know that I tried to help you as much as I could, but I was just a small innocent child. I tried to tell dad to stop hurting you, and he promised he would stop but he broke that promise too many times. I felt guilty for loving him when he hurt you so much, but he was my dad and nothing could change that.

I emerged from my childhood traumatised and confused about love. I lost the love I had for myself somewhere along the way. I don't know when or where but it has been gone for such a long time.

I tried to help as much as I could but I was just a child. I did not know what to do nor did I have any understanding of what was happening. I tried to help you by cleaning the house on the Saturdays and then I became very independent. I did that because I thought it would alleviate your busy stressful life. I knew how hard you worked.

I thought my independence would make you happy and proud of me. You don't know how important it was for me to have you say that you were proud of me. I don't think you understood what I needed and I could not explain because I did not know either. I just kept doing what I thought I needed to do to help you.

It was my strategy to survive. I never wanted to feel that fear again. I never wanted you to suffer at the hands of my father ever again, but I loved my father. I tried to help you so that you and dad did not argue. I loved you and you never knew or understood how it broke my heart to see you crying.

I want to tell you that I know that you were doing your very best you knew how with the resources that you had.

You taught me so much and you were so generous with your willingness to share your mistakes with me. This helped me in my life and made me the person I am today. I am strong and resilient, and I thank you for that but it is time for me to forgive myself for not being able to help you.

I have spent my whole life avoiding conflict and confrontation because in my childhood this led to violence. I have just realised that I do not need to protect myself from conflict and confrontation anymore because I can speak out for myself. I lost my voice because I associated speaking out with violence, yet as an adult I could defend myself. I could not defend myself as a child.

I tried so hard to please you and that I went about my life trying to achieve as many things as I possibly could each time waiting for your approval. It never came and therefore I just kept trying harder and harder. Each time I had an achievement in my life, I waited for your approval but it never came, so then I would just work harder to achieve more. I never stopped to celebrate any achievements because I believed that every time I achieved something, I lost the most important things in my life. You were the most important person in my life and I lost you and I don't know why. 'Where did you go?' 'Why weren't you there for me when I was out there doing what I thought that you wanted?'.

I don't celebrate things in my life because I associate achievement with loss and rejection. When I married a wonderful man, I lost you. When I had my first beautiful daughter, I lost you. When my father died, I lost you both.

I went on to associate achievement with rejection, loss, and abandonment therefore this created the fear for me to push forward in my life.

I did not get what my driving force was until I joined the police service and I realised that the messages that I was so gracious to accept from strangers just did not match what was in my head.

The strength that you gave me helped me to seek out happiness but this came with the loss of my own family. Again, I could not celebrate my achievement because this just reinforced my loss and gave me the evidence that achievement was nothing to celebrate.

I have been torn for so long. The skills that you gave me in my life have helped me to survive. The lessons I learnt as a child in order to survive have not done me justice as an adult because I have clung on to them. Whenever life got tough or sticky, I reverted back to those survival skills I developed as a child to remain safe. I give them up now and retire them. Those beliefs no longer serve me. I can stand alone without them and I can defend myself. I want my voice back and I want to celebrate my achievements.

I felt that I lost you when I got married. I wanted you to be so happy for me because I listened to you. I did not make the same mistakes as you always told me, but I felt that I lost you at that point and you stepped back from my life at a time when I wanted you in my life.

I have missed having you in my life but I felt you left me no choice. I felt I had to protect my children and that is why I have not allowed you to be part of their lives. I make no apologies for that. I want to tell you mum, that I have always loved you and I have found forgiveness. I hope that you have to.

Chapter 40

Domestic Violence—
An Undesirable Prerequisite

> This chapter is written from my personal perspective and in no way represents the views or policies of either the NSW Police or DOCS (the Department of Community Services).

I did not want to admit to being a victim of domestic violence as a child and it has only been in recent times that I have been more open to talking about it. I must say though, that my own personal experience gave me added knowledge during my employment in the police service when I was dealing with victims of domestic violence.

On a personal level, my time as a police officer gave me some insight into what my mother may have been experiencing in her attempts to break away from my father.

The laws were very different in the late sixties and the issue of domestic violence was just that 'domestic'. Police had little powers in relation to the offenders unless the victim was willing to cooperate. This was unlikely because it meant airing problems on the home front in public. There was a lot of shame and guilt placed upon the victims if they spoke out.

My mother told me recently that the police sergeant who attended our house that frightening day had said to my mother, 'Put your husband to bed and stop antagonising him'. Thank goodness, this would not happen in our current environment.

I can only have admiration for the fact that my mother had made an attempt to leave my father because during those times it would be frowned upon. I can only imagine how difficult it was to cart five children between the ages of five and fifteen, fourteen hours on a train to Brisbane. One can only think that she was desperate to get away and start fresh.

Just as the laws were inadequate in the late sixties, so were the resources to assist mothers fleeing violent homes. Even though my mother made an attempt to leave the violence, she returned so that she could provide food and shelter for us. She showed great courage but like so many domestic violence victims, she fell into the mindset that the offender will change and the break had taught them a lesson.

I want to point out that I do not class myself as an expert in domestic violence and I am no longer a serving member of the NSW police. I would just like to share my experience.

I became aware as a police officer that one of the biggest issues confronting domestic violence victims was safe accommodation. At the time police become involved in a domestic dispute the victims commonly expressed concerns about their ability to provide a safe and secure place for themselves and particularly their children. Under the current NSW domestic violence legislation, police have greater powers than anytime previously. Police can remove the offender without cooperation from the victim if they have fears for the safety of the victim/victims.

I used my police powers under the legislation on many occasions but in some instances removing the offender, unintentionally forced the victims into further difficulties. It is one thing for police to remove the offender or aggressor but it is a whole other issue for the victim to just pack up the home environment and find somewhere safe to go. I dealt with many offenders of domestic violence that just 'never get it'. They blame alcohol, drugs, poverty, 'the system', their job, their boss, their wife, their partner, their childhood, their parents, their children, the house, the dog, the car and anything else that may take the blame away from themselves. I attended domestic related incidents with victims and offenders from all walks of life. Some lived in multimillion dollar homes right through to housing department, caravans, and the homeless. I attended jobs where the relationships varied from sibling rivalry, same sex couples, defacto relationship, husband and wife, parents and children, flatmates etc.

Domestic violence is happening in all suburbs, in all areas of the community. Unlike my mother's experience, today there are community-based resources available and even though they may be somewhat stretched at different times they are at least available. There are many underlying reasons why domestic violence victims return to the same situation time and time again. One of those reasons is low self-esteem and a feeling that they deserve what is dished out by the offenders. Another reason is that women live in fear continuously and are too scared to flee the violence because they are afraid that this will enrage the perpetrator even further and therefore escalate the violence. The cycle of violence continues in many cases because of the fear involved and the victims have been made to feel powerless to make changes. My father did not change; he was just better behaved for a short period until the arguments started again and after he had been drinking.

My father was an alcoholic and did have some mental health issues at different times throughout his life. I don't believe he ever wanted to stop drinking even if it meant losing his family. It was not until after my parent's divorce and he was in his sixties that he chose something more important than alcohol. My father was invited by my mother to return to her home (not the relationship), but he was not allowed to consume alcohol under any circumstances. My father made that choice and I was told that he was a different person and everything was going well. Unfortunately it was a short time later that he became sick and died. I found it interesting that he could make that choice and stick to it. I believe he finally made one of the best decisions of his life.

I am of course not the only adult victim of domestic violence suffered during childhood, but I have chosen to speak out and make people aware that children are the innocent victims.

I believe parents do not understand the full impact abuse can have on a child. Even if the child is not abused themselves, they can be just as traumatised seeing their mother suffer. I am a testament to that. In NSW we have the Department of Community Services who attempts to look after the best interests of children and families.

As a society we cannot leave it solely up to an organisation to protect our children. Our children are our future and if they are damaged as an adult because of abuse they witnessed or suffered as a child then where does that leave the generations to come. The abuse within my family was generational, handed down from one generation to the other. My personal view is that it can be stopped in its tracks by education, resources, and support. My mother believed that that was all she deserved because she was made to feel like that after the abuse she suffered at the hands of her mother and father. If as a society we are attempting to support our children, we must educate the parents in the effects domestic violence has on our children and in return support them to seek assistance to stop the violence.

As a police officer, I was talking to a domestic violence victim about what had happened to her. The victim started to explain what her partner had done. She grabbed her throat to demonstrate to me the nature of the assault. At this time, her five-year-old child came from another room, interrupted us, and said, 'No mummy, daddy was like this' The child placed his hands around his mother's neck, turned his innocent facial expression into an angry grimace, and grabbed the victim's throat in a similar fashion to what the child had seen his father do. I was taken back with the intensity in which the child mirrored his father's actions.

I understand why the laws relating to domestic violence in NSW (today) were refined and why mandatory reporting of children at risk came into play. As my brothers and sisters and I got older it was easier to remove ourselves from the house when arguments would get heated.

Young children don't have that ability to remove themselves so they rely on their main caregivers to shield them. It was my older sister who cared for me, but who was caring for her because she was also a child.

I know the NSW Police do a great job because I was one of them, but the fact is that the police or Department of Community Services (DOCS) cannot protect the victims twenty-four hours a day. Even if they pitched a tent in the backyard, they still could not guarantee 100 per cent protection. We have to as a community work out a way to empower the victims to say no to violence and we have to come down even harder on the offenders. We have to say no to their excuses and make them take responsibility for themselves.

The parents involved in these situations must also at some point stand up and take responsibility for their own selves and their children. I don't expect you to go it alone; I only ask that you seek help. Our job as a community is to support them in their attempts to break free of the violence and abuse. My mother returned to my father because of lack of resources in the 1960s, but we are living in the year 2012 and times are different.

At least as a police officer, we could break the cycle of violence by removing one party for short periods and sometimes that was enough to assist the victims to make some changes.

My policing experience with domestic violence victims showed me that after a period of time, the victim's start to believe they are deserving of the violence because they feel they have done something wrong or it was their fault. Their self-esteem is often at an all time low due to frequent verbal abuse and ongoing physical abuse. The offenders become masters of manipulation and have all the power and control over their victims. The victims can see no way out of the cycle of violence or abuse so therefore the cycle just keeps repeating itself. If you are reading this book and you know someone who is a victim of domestic violence then do what you can to offer them support. Even if it is as simple as writing down one of the help line phone numbers in the back of this book and giving it to them. If we all did a little bit then hopefully the little bits will add up and make a difference.

Over the many years I have worked in the emergency environment as a nurse I have seen several victims who presented with injuries inflicted by their intimate partners. However, I have also seen those whom I suspect are victims of domestic violence but for whatever reason have chosen not to disclose that. We must ask ourselves 'what can we do to encourage people to seek support and not live in secrecy?'

In no way is this chapter meant to be an exhaustive perspective on the issues relating to domestic violence but just my personal view encompassing my experience both personally and professionally. The one murder that I attended was enough for me to question what we are doing as a society and what the government is doing to try and reduce the numbers of domestic violence victims and homicides. I wrote this book to help others by sharing my thoughts and experiences. If I can get through to one person and improve their life or the lives of their children then I will continue to have hope that we can do something to reduce violence in our society.

CHAPTER 41

HISTORY CAN REPEAT ITSELF—IF WE LET IT

> Don't be a victim of your history, be a master of your future.
> (Unknown)

In 2012 the world is a very different place to what it was when my parents were growing up and even more so when their own parents were growing up. We inherit from our families the generational influences of the era in which they were born. My parents were born in the 1920/30s and their parents were born in the late 1800s and early 1900s. It's not hard to figure out that life was very different in those times.

My mother used to speak to us about the treatment of unmarried mothers and societies attitude towards them. The depression impacted on the lives of families and times were very tough. It was a harsh society and nothing like we would know today.

I believe it is important for children to know what influenced their parents and how that has impacted their child rearing.

Knowledge about society's norms whilst you were a child can create better understanding of the 'why' things happened to you. It is not an excuse of course but it provides you a better idea of 'what the hell were my parent's thinking?'.

When I was trying to understand the difficulties my parents were having in their relationship, it certainly helped to know a little about where they came from. I know that my parents did not deliberately set out to create a volatile unstable upbringing for us, but that was no consolation when it has affected me for most of my life.

I think as a child we mirror those people who we have closest to us. They are our peers, mentors, and our idols regardless of the how screwed up they may seem to be. It is probably reasonable to say (from my experience) that we as children and young adults will pick up the more dominant emotions that we observe. If the more dominant emotions are negative then that is what we will take on. We may also perceive these emotions or messages in a manner that may not be the reality. Throughout childhood we have to become adaptable to every situation to enable our survival and self-preservation. The boundaries and guidelines throughout my childhood were ever changing and therefore confusing.

In learning these lessons at fifty-one years of age, I am now able to continue letting go of my past and I can now understand that the acceptance I sought from my parents was never going to come to fruition. I have learnt that the acceptance that I have been looking for all my life does not come from an external source but from inside of me. It is ourselves that must create our own happiness because no one else can do it for you and no one else knows you better than you do.

It is far too easy to look back on your life and with hindsight think of different choices you could have made. I can see that I would have gone in some different direction but whilst you are living in real time it is hard to be objective.

I asked myself 'Why did all those things happen to me?'

'Why did I feel like I did not have access to my own father?' 'Why did I allow people to have so much power over me' and 'why did I think that I could not speak out'.

I searched for these answers many times during my life but I could never really find them. It was not until the foundations of my life as I knew it fell from under me and my raw emotions became exposed that I was able to slowly piece together what had happened to the pearl inside me. At this time I started the slow journey to self-awareness and took a good hard look at my past and the programming that set my future on a path of self loathing and a feeling of being unworthy of anything good in my life.

I agree that the bad stuff is so much easier to believe but I have come to the realisation that speaking out against something that does not appear right can help start to change our beliefs.

I lost the ability to vocalise my desires and my thoughts to the point I nearly did not see my father in his dying moments. I realise now that everyone needs to have a voice and it is up to us to make sure that someone listens.

The decision I made in regard to the care of my children came from my experience as a child and young adult. I had learnt enough from my past and my professional experience both nursing and policing that helped me to make the best decision for my children's care.

This was a distinct moment in breaking away from my past and pivotal in redirecting the generational patterns and messages that had been so prominent in my own childhood. I made a conscious decision to create a positive environment for my children, and I am very proud of that.

CHAPTER 42

THE GIFT OF A NEW BEGINNING—
THE GIFT IS TO MYSELF

> Though no one can go back and make a brand new start, anyone can start from now and make a brand new beginning
>
> (Carl Bard)

Sometimes I wished that I could have taken a pencil rubber to the parts of my life that caused me so much pain and just erase them from my memory. Imagine if we could start a day with a clean slate every now and then. Wouldn't that be great for all of us? *Or* would it?

Let's face it, everyone has cringe moments. We would like to forget the times we feel remorse for something we have said or done. I believe remorse is like an internal regulator that gives us an indication that we are obeying our own value system. It nudges our conscience and reminds us who we are. Unfortunately we are designed to learn by our experiences and not just the good ones but the bad ones as well. In fact, I believe we learn more lessons from our bad experiences than anything else.

The mistakes we make and the pain and hardships that we cause or endure during our life are what teach us our greatest lessons. These lessons help us to grow as an individual and propel us towards becoming the type of person we aspire to be so erasing them is not a valid option.

I have been told by several people that I am a strong person and I know myself, that my strength and resilience are the reason I am still here today. I survived that night when I saw my police issued firearm as a way out of life. I survived the battle of the relentless lapping waves of my depression. I rode the emotional roller coaster after separation and endured the grief and loss I felt for those loved ones lost. I am so proud of myself that I got through it but I will never forget the times when I did not feel so strong. In fact, I felt so weak that I could easily be broken.

The moments I felt my weakest were the times when the lessons I needed to learn were staring me right in the face. I just had to wade through the emotional barriers to stay awake to them, listen to them, process them and absorb them. When something stares you in the face you have only two choices, one to ignore it and the other to hit it front on. I chose to hit them front on.

Hitting something front on and taking small steps forward sometimes meant, I had to admit to myself that I was playing the victim. It was much easier though to lay blame on others for my circumstances or become stuck in the moment unwilling or unable to take the next step. It was not easy to admit to myself that I stuffed up in some areas of my life or made bad choices.

During these times it helped me to spend some time in solitude so I could search for answers in an attempt to uncover the underlying message. There was no point believing you are being shown a lesson when you can't or fail to interpret it. It was at the moment I interpreted the lesson that I could take another step forward. I was determined to leave no stone unturned.

I am living my second half of a century and I want it to be exceptional. I had not suffered so much pain and adversity to just settle for an OK future it had to be exceptional. There was no alternative for me. At my fiftieth birthday, I said to my friends that the first fifty years of my life had been a practice for me and the next fifty years were when all the lessons and experiences come together. Like a crescendo! I wanted my birthday to be a turning point for change, and it did not matter how long it was going to take me but I just knew I wanted to start living again. For me, that meant being the true me and living life with authenticity and integrity.

My police training had little to do with my inability to acknowledge the positive messages I received throughout my adult life. It was the people that I met during the training that equipped me with the information which created the catalyst for change. I needed to make a start somewhere and when the penny literally dropped, the ripple effect exploded. It was time to stop the messages from the past from having control over the way I lived today. The patterns and habits I established from early childhood no longer served their purpose so why would I just keep hanging on to them.

Everything that has happened to me in the past I see as a gift. The lessons of life have empowered me, the people I've met have enlightened me, and the adversities have given me strength and resilience.

I believe the most important thing for all of us is to keep listening and learning. I have listened and that has helped me restring my pearls. Once I get that right, I believe everything else will fall into place.

When I go to work as a nurse I don't just see patients I see real people with real lives but sometimes they are so ill that they are not going to live another day. What do you think they would do for a second chance at life? I say anything, but life does not always give us a second chance.

What I have tried to relay to my readers about my lessons may seem less important when you read stories of people close to death, but this is our life and one day we will be the ones close to death. If your own adversities are holding you back from living your authentic life then you owe it to yourself and everyone around you to find your true happiness. We don't know when it will be our turn to look death in the eye.

My past had been so dysfunctional for me it was like dragging around a giant ball and chain that I just could not bring myself to sever. The previous attempts I made to break free had failed but this time I had sacrificed time with my children. I owed it to the three of us to change my future and find freedom otherwise that precious time I spent without them was meaningless.

My thoughts relating to my past are spoken perfectly by the character Simba, the lion, in Walt Disney's classic, The Lion King. In the movie there is a scene where Simba meets the baboon named Rafiki. They talk about Mufasa who was Simba's father. Simba feels the pain of his past and the loss of his father and it is stopping him from moving forward as he would have done. At that time Rafiki hits Simba over the head with his cane. Simba says,

'What did you do that for?' Rafiki replies, 'It doesn't matter, it is in the past'. Simba rubs his head and says, 'Yeah! But it still hurts'.

'How true that is?' The past can hurt a lot. Rafiki goes on to say, 'Oh yes the past can hurt but the way I see it, you can run from it or learn from it'.

We are all humans and therefore have skeletons in our closet but each one of us is unique. I believe every one of us has a story to tell and we have all lived through our own adversities. Not one story can be any better or worse than another because each story is unique to the person it belongs to.

I wrote my story because it was an important part of my healing process and a way to seek forgiveness from those important people who have been in my life. I learnt from my writing that before I can forgive others, I needed to forgive myself and it was time.

I know that my life will always be full of lessons and adversities, but I look forward to it because I have restored my belief in myself. I believe that I am just as wonderful as the person next to me and I deserve everything in life that comes to me. The resources I needed to confront life's challenges don't come from external sources but from within us. It is the support that we seek from others that helps us to unleash those resources. It was my willingness to search out the support I felt I needed that has assisted me to navigate the roller coaster instead of believing I was imprisoned by it.

In the final days that lead up to the completion of my book, I decided to take myself away from my laptop and go outside for some badly needed fresh air. I wanted to reflect on what I had written and just absorb the fact that writing this book had helped me to get through the challenges in my life.

I walked at a comfortable pace around the neighbourhood as I had done on many occasions throughout my writing journey. I thought it was befitting to take a different route. The completion of my story was a significant moment and a change of direction would give me a new point of reference to my future.

I noticed the vibrant flowers, their fragrances, and picturesque display splattered amongst the well-manicured lawns. As I walked, I listened to my Ipod playing some of the music that helped me through my darkest times. I noticed the lyrics had a different meaning to me from what they had when I first listened to them.

Twenty minutes into my walk, I came to an intersection that was unfamiliar to me. I stood and looked to see where the roads would take me and I contemplated which direction to take. I was drawn like a magnet to turning left and going in the opposite direction to my home.

I walked about 100 metres and came across a children's play area with a swing positioned in an open area taking pride of place in front of the play equipment. The grass was bright green and the late afternoon sun was beaming brightly through the branches of the large tree that shaded the equipment. It was a beautiful sight.

I continued walking, but the vision of the swing created an overwhelming need for me to turn back and take a seat on the swing.

I sat down and started to propel myself forward and backward. I felt at ease with the swing and just kept trying to propel myself harder so I could experience the motion and feel the wind in my face.

I waited for my mind to start spinning with the thoughts of my life but instead I felt an unfamiliar silence. I felt content and peaceful and this paved the way for me to enjoy the moment on the swing.

I took my thoughts back to my childhood swing but to my surprise I was happy that I could not recreate that same carefree moment in time. Instead, I felt overwhelmed with joy that I had created something even better. I leaned my body back to increase the momentum and intensity of the swinging sensation and I felt the tears start to stream down my face. I realised that I have given myself the gift of a new beginning and I could embrace the child within me just as I could the valuable lessons I had learnt along the way. I had nurtured the pearl inside me back to its natural form and now it was time for me to embrace my new beginning.

I could not stop myself smiling and yet I was not really sure why. I had no thoughts in my head other than a feeling of being free to swing. My head was no longer spinning dizzily with the worries of life and the burden of the past. I felt liberated and free. At that moment I recognised that I had travelled through life in the hard lane, and I was a survivor. I sat and enjoyed the motion of the swing, back and forward. I leaned my body back to a horizontal position just like I did as a child on the swing my father so lovingly made. The tears just kept running and I knew from that moment that I had created my new beginning. I felt excitement and gratitude for everything that I had experienced. I thought of those people in my life who I shared so much with and I felt blessed with love and forgiveness for them and I hoped too that they can find forgiveness for me.

I walked home with a skip in my step.

The completion of this book represents a new beginning for me. It was an eerie coincidence that around the same time, I was putting the last chapters together. Kelly Clarkson's latest album was about to be released.

Of course, I was going to buy it and when I did, I was taken aback by the irony of track two called Stronger. I can resonate with the words just like I did with breakaway especially 'What doesn't kill you makes you stronger, stand a little taller, doesn't mean I am lonely when I am alone' 'What doesn't kill you makes a fighter' footsteps even lighter. Doesn't mean I'm over 'cause your gone'. 'What doesn't kill you makes you stronger, just me, myself, and I'.

I could not think of a more appropriate way to finish this book knowing that I am stronger for what I have experienced and that breaking away was worth it.

IMPORTANT PHONE NUMBERS AND RESOURCES

Holmes and Rahe Stress Scale referenced from Wikipedia
Referred to in text.

Domestic Violence Line
1800 656 463

Dads in Distress
1300 853 437
www.dadsindistress.asn.au

Rape Crisis Centre
1800 424 017
www.nswrapecrisis.com.au

Family Services Australia
1300 365 859

Kids Helpline
1800 551 800
www.kidshelp.com.au

Lifeline
131 114
www.lifeline.org.au

SANE Mental Illness Helpline
1800 187 263 www.sane.org

Mensline Australia
1300 789 978

Family Relationship Advice line
1800 050 321

Suicide Call Back Service (National)
1300 659 467
www.suicidecallbackservice.org.au

Beyond Blue Info line
1300 224 636
www.beyondblue.org.au

Black Dog Institute
www.blackdoginstitute.org.au

Mental Health First Aid
www.mhfa.com.au

Mental Health Council of Australia
www.mhca.org.au

Salvo Care Line
1300 363 622
www.salvos.org.au

Victims Support Line
1800 633 063
www.lawlink.nsw.gov.au/vs

Gay &Lesbian Counselling Line
8594 9596
www.glcsnsw.org.au

St Vincent de Paul Society
www.vinnies.org.au

Anglicare
www.anglicare.org.au
13 26 22

Department of Community Services
www.community.nsw.gov.au
13 21 11